NO RISK INVOLVED

NO RISK INVOLVED

The Ken McGinley Story:
Survivor of a Nuclear Experiment

Ken McGinley
and Eamonn P. O'Neill

MAINSTREAM
PUBLISHING

First published in Great Britain 1991 by
MAINSTREAM PUBLISHING COMPANY (EDINBURGH) LTD
7 Albany Street
Edinburgh EH1 3UG

British Library Cataloguing in Publication Data
McGinley, Ken
 No Risk Involved.
 1. Line Islands. Hydrogen bombs. Testing by Great Britain,
 history – Biographies
 I. Title II. O'Neill, Eamonn P.
 623.45119092

 ISBN 1–85158–337–8

Typeset by Falcon Typographic Art Ltd, Edinburgh and London
Printed in Great Britain by Mackays of Chatham Ltd

To Alice and Louise,
for their patience, understanding and,
above all, love,
from Ken.

Introduction and Acknowledgments

I FIRST MET Ken McGinley in 1989 when I was researching several lengthy articles on the British Nuclear Test Veterans Association. As fate would have it most of these pieces were never printed by the newspapers I offered them to. Explanations for these decisions varied. I was deeply disappointed and felt that I had in some way let Ken McGinley and his association down since most of the information in my articles came from Ken who had spent almost seven years gathering his material from all over the world. I failed to understand why the majority of the UK media, especially the newspapers, had not despatched someone to spend some time looking into the claims which Ken made. When I told Ken that my articles had been turned down by the newspapers (although in one case I was paid for my work despite the fact that it wasn't used), he asked me over to his house. "Why don't you write a book with me?" he asked. I considered this proposal briefly before deciding that Ken and his cause were a story waiting to be written. Within one week of this offer I had secured a contract from Mainstream Publishing in Edinburgh.

Over a period of almost six months I practically moved in with Ken McGinley, his wife Alice and daughter Louise. I spent hours wading through the documentary material he has gathered since 1982 and accompanied him on countless journeys throughout the UK in his capacity as chairman of the BNTVA. Towards the end of the project we spent memorable nights in a chilly caravan on the outskirts of Ken's favourite second home, Dunoon, in an attempt to make some sense out of the complex arguments surrounding the nuclear tests of the 1950s and 1960s. Night after night I read the mountains of letters which Ken receives from ordinary faceless people who believe their lives have been permanently changed because a husband, a brother or a father participated in the bomb-tests. I spent long hours chatting to many of these

7

people, a harrowing but strangely rewarding experience that I'll never forget.

This book could not have been written without the help of all the people, past and present, who have contributed to the BNTVA. The association relies on membership fees and the odd donation to survive in an increasingly harsh economic climate. All the members display an extraordinary degree of quiet dignity, a very rare quality which is often conspicuous only by its absence in my generation. Some names stand out in my memory so I would like to say a personal thanks to the following: John Hall, Peter Fletcher, M. Reid, Ken Taylor, Mike Doyle, Cyril Hawkins and family, Phill Munn and the wonderfully brave Frank and Sheila Gray. Thanks must also go to a unique lady who opened her door and her heart to me on a very wet winter's night – June Robinson. This book is, in part, dedicated to all of these special people.

I would also like to extend my appreciation to the following individuals: all the MPs who have championed the cause of the BNTVA over the years, especially, David Alton, Kevin MacNamara, Winston Churchill, BNTVA patron Jack Ashley, Tam Dayell and last but not least, Bob Clay; the staff of the *Glasgow Herald* and *Daily Record* clippings-libraries for their patience and good humour; Professor Tom M. Devine, Dr J. H. Treble, Dr Simon L. Adams, Dr Hamish Fraser, Dr Bill Wurthman, and Sheriff Colin McGregor (retired).

Gerry Keenan deserves a special mention for being a real oasis in what appeared to be an academic and artistic desert. Thanks, all those long chats were not wasted . . . sir!

Blair Jenkins and David Scott at Scottish Television must be thanked for their professionalism and judgement. Their unstinting faith in this project was truly appreciated. Paul Murricane and Ross Wilson, both from Scottish Television, contributed greatly to the fabric of this text. The former must be thanked for sharing his wealth of knowledge with a precocious young journalist who thought he knew it all and the latter must be mentioned for generally putting up with the same precocious young journalist who suddenly started to lose the rag when he realised that he didn't know half as much as he thought he did! So Paul and Ross – genuine thanks from the "Staff" . . .

This book would never have seen the light of day without the support of Bill Campbell, one of the directors of Mainstream Publishing Company, Edinburgh. His unfailing patience and guidance, especially during our memorable first meeting, was one of the most pleasant surprises that this journalist has ever come across in his professional career, and I would also like to thank Penny, Alison and everyone "upstairs" for all their help in this project.

At a more personal level I would like to thank my parents for daring to encourage individuality and excellence amid a sea of conformity and mediocrity. They never failed to provide me with the two most important gifts a son could ever want – wisdom and love. I love you both.

Sympathetic ears during this project were provided by Jim and Meg Scullion from Coatbridge – two needles which I happened upon in the proverbial haystack. I owe them. A special mention for special reasons is also given to Ms Sarah D. Sterling, from the original "little upheaval".

These acknowledgements wouldn't be complete without mentioning five very special ladies: Bernadette, Patricia, Kathleen, Geraldine and Theresa. All of these wonderful human beings were there in the beginning and I hope they all stick around for the finale "'cos you ain't seen nothin' yet!"

Lastly, I would like to pay tribute to Ken McGinley. I've read thousands and thousands of words about this man, by journalists from every corner of the globe. Nearly all of these articles refer to him as a "victim" of nuclear tests. I disagree with this. I've spent hours with this individual and have came to know him as a man and a friend. Therefore, I feel qualified to take this opportunity to place on record the following observation; Ken McGinley is no victim, on the contrary, he is in a very real sense, one thing and one thing only . . . a hero. God bless.

Eamonn P. O'Neill,
1991

Chapter One

THEY TELL ME that my Granda was a right old bugger. He was Irish born and bred from Strabane in County Tyrone. My own father was a tough-nut as well. He went away to fight in the army in the First World War when he was only fifteen years old. When he came back to Johnstone, the town near Glasgow where the family have always lived, he started boxing in the boxing-booths that used to come around this area. They were rough places. Wee, thin boxers would be paraded out in front of the crowd at the beginning of the evening for everyone to see. The local crowd were usually well tanked-up and they would laugh at the size of the under-nourished-looking specimens that stood in front of them wearing those baggy shorts that made them look even thinner. Little did they know that this was exactly what they were supposed to be thinking. They were, in fact, simply being lulled into a false sense of security. The old barker who was running the show then grandly proceeded to offer a few quid to anyone who was prepared to go a few rounds with them. Sure enough, some big, heavy and clumsy local would be daft enough to rise to the bait. Inevitably, the huffing and puffing local hero would be carried for the first two rounds by the small professional so that his pals in the crowd thought that they were getting their money's worth. The third round was always the last. By that time the big fella had thrown all the punches in the book and was really starting to get tired. The wee, professional pugilist would wait for the right opening and suddenly go to work on him. Nine out of ten times the bouts ended with you-know-who being carried out of the ring at the end of the round . . . feet-first!

My father often told us stories about seven-and-a-half-stone flyweights taking fourteen stone blow-hards apart, cutting their puffy features to pieces with lightning jabs. It's no wonder that it was these booths, during the same period, that gave birth to Scotland's very first world champion boxer, Benny Lynch. And he was a flyweight! Anyway my father was a regular at the booths and he must have been good because he earned himself a proper booth-name, which was something of an honour in those days. He fought under the rather exotic guise of "The Fighting American". God only knows why they called him that – everyone that saw him knew fine well he was wee Jimmy McGinley from Johnstone. Still, I suppose it succeeded in bringing a bit of colour into someone's drab wee life at a time when the whole world seemed to be in the throws of an economic depression. My dad's most stable job was as a stoker with a local engineering firm. The heavy work there along with the boxing-training meant that he was built like the side of a house, despite the fact that he couldn't have stood more than five feet two inches tall.

From time to time there were arguments in the family and as you might expect most of them centred around our lack of money. There was a whole squad of us living in a three-apartment council house in Johnstone at the beginning of the 1940s when I was only two years old. It was one of those two-storey houses that were built during the inter-war years as a result of intense political lobbying by the public at the end of the First World War when they were determined to have "Homes fit for Heroes" to live in. It seemed like a palace to us at the time and indeed the quality of the house must have been good since thousands of a similar design are still inhabited throughout Scotland. Living with me in the house when I was a child were my parents, brothers John, Danny, Davie, Alister and Jimmy, and sisters Nancy and Dorothy. My grandfather and Uncle Danny were liable to make unannounced, colourful appearances from time to time. The latter will always remain in my mind as a big man who wore a kilt on the day that the Second World War ended, who occasionally reeked of beer and who was always willing to start a fight at the drop of a hat. Many a night Uncle Danny would come reeling through our bedroom door when we were all asleep, get down on his knees beside one of us and launch into "Danny Boy". The McGinley family house was, to put it mildly, a bit on the busy side.

At one point my father was unemployed, on and off, for about nine years. He even walked to Fort William looking for work, that's how bad things were. He did wee odd jobs like cleaning out the drains at the local butchers in return for a parcel containing link-sausages and liver. To the onlooker he must have seemed like an ideal husband and father, since he was always taking one of us out for a walk in the pram. He would park it beside a local turnip field and nip behind the hedge while the occupant of the pram looked as innocent as hell. Two minutes later he would re-emerge from behind the hedge, with a load of turnips under his arm for my mother to use in the soup. I suppose it's almost laughable now but it shows how hard up we really were and the frightening thing is that there were a lot of families worse off than us at that time.

The whole family went to the local Roman Catholic school in Johnstone, St Margaret's. My first class at school was a sight for sore eyes. The most lasting image was the dress code. All the kids wore sand-shoes in the winter and wellingtons in the summer . . . it was crazy! We got our feet soaked right through at the worst end of the year, then we all had red rims around our calf-muscles from the edge of the wellies rubbing during the summer. Uniforms were a precarious affair, with everyone dressing according to their means. I went to school in a variety of different outfits, the quality of each depending on my father's employment status at that particular time. Sometimes he would work in somebody's garden and as part of the payment he would be given some second-hand clothes for the family or else he would bring some clothes from the Parish reserves that were held for the local poor.

There were actually three different schools within the red sandstone walls of St Margaret's and you were supposed to progress through them as you got older and wiser . . . well that was the theory. The population in the area was booming, which is in total contrast with the situation that exists in many parts of the country today. We had never heard of the phrase "Falling Class-Registers"; in fact, in my very first class there were roughly eighty children, meaning the whole intake had to be split into two groups on the day we arrived.

That morning I was accompanied to the school gates by my big sister, Nancy. (In my mother's absence it was Nancy who did all the "looking after". On a Sunday night, for example, the whole lot of us would kneel down in front of her so that she could check all our heads for lice before we went back to school on the Monday morning. Nowadays that might sound a bit extreme or melodramatic but I'm telling you the story because I know for a fact that every other family in the area was going through exactly the same process at exactly the same time!) When I walked into what seemed like a massive classroom, the very first thing that grabbed my attention was a rocking-horse and a swing-boat, which both sat in front of the teacher's desk. They were painted in bright, fantastic colours and to my young eyes they seemed to be bordering on the magical. My background meant that my contact with proper toys was

13

minimal, so I was desperate to have a go on either of them straight away. But there was just one wee smelly problem, a problem that would make an unwelcome appearance every morning for the next year, a problem delivered by each and every member of that class at one time or another. The horse and the boat, you see, were treated as the unofficial class toilet . . . . Perhaps it was the fact that you sat down in a comfortable seat when you played on them; perhaps it was the excitement of having half-decent toys for a change; perhaps it was the sheer frustration of glancing over your shoulder and seeing thirty-nine pairs of eyes ready to kill you stone-dead if you dared to rock for another second; or perhaps it was the vigorous rocking-motion required by each toy that did it, who knows? But, whatever the mysterious cause behind the pool or pile in the boat or on the rocking-horse's saddle, it always seemed to be me that sat on or in it! I have to admit though that I was the perpetrator of the said criminal act on at least one occasion. On that particular morning the root of my bowel problem could be traced back to too much milk in the porridge that I had eaten for my breakfast. After I'd rocked and shat to my heart's contentment the teacher dragged me out in front of the class. My trousers stuck to my backside with something not unlike a layer of wet cement. After what seemed like an eternal time-lapse my sister Nancy appeared at the classroom door with a beaming red face and full of apologies to the teacher who had probably heard them all a thousand times before.

I was hauled home with my ear getting a good clout every hundred of yards or so. The trousers had to be scraped clean then washed, meanwhile I was given the whole day off school. There was no way that I could be sent back after that happened, not because of the embarrassment or shame but due to the fact that my trousers had to be steeped in disinfectant for a few hours. They were, you see, the only pair that I owned.

I was at primary school during the mid-years of the Second World War. In Scotland, the war didn't seem to touch our lives much. But perhaps it did and I just don't remember too much about it. One year that does stand out in my mind, however, is 1942. My brother Jimmy fell ill with a sore throat during the summer of that year. He was a lovely boy with dark, dark curly hair that sat on a wee handsome face. His condition worsened in the July so he was rushed into the Royal Alexandria Infirmary in the nearest big town, Paisley. I can still remember very clearly the day that he was taken away in the ambulance. All the family were due to go and see Walt Disney's *Dumbo* that night but the outing was cancelled. Within a matter of hours the decision was taken to remove Jimmy's tonsils. During the operation the surgeon made some kind of basic mistake – my mother was told that one of the sharp medical instruments had slipped – with the result being my big brother suffered heavy bleeding. He died on the operating table. He was only ten years old.

After Jimmy's death my mother approached the surgeon. She questioned the circumstances surrounding her son's passing. "Why had such a basic operation gone wrong?" She was told that she should go home and forget about him since "she had plenty of other children to look after". Furthermore, the family should forget any notions of trying to claim compensation due to the fact that we would never be able to afford all the expensive legal fees. At the time all she could utter to the heartless person that told her this was: "I am not an animal." The memory of this particular incident has always stayed with me. It underlines how the authorities often believe they have the God-given right to step into innocent people's lives and, on their terms, attempt to alter them for good without any kind of comeback. But when you try to restore the balance and seek justice they will always use your lack of know-how, or lack of money which could buy the know-how, to keep you in your place. But over the years I've managed to put this bitterness to good use. I've had to deal with so-called "faceless bureaucrats" from time to time, making me realise that they do have a face and that they can all be held accountable for their actions if you have the resources, the patience and the burning desire to see justice served.

The local woods were located near our house. On Sundays my brothers and I used to go there to saw up trees into logs for firewood. When we had finished chopping and sawing, we would pile the heavy logs on to the barrow as high as possible before carting the whole lot back home. The woods also housed Johnstone Castle which served as a prisoner-of-war camp during that period. My brother Davie and I used to take jam sandwiches from our house up to the fences around the camp and pass them through the wire to the Italian and German prisoners. Sometimes I would be called over to the fence by one of them. He would carefully purse his lips and gesture with his fingers to me in a conspiratorial manner. You didn't have to be a genius to realise that he was desperate for a cigarette, so I would run like the wind, back through the woods to our house and steal a few of my father's Woodbines for him.

Sometimes the guards around the compound would be changed so they would march right through the town, where the entire population would turn out to watch. On other occasions it was the prisoners that were moved using the same process. I remember one night the town witnessed the arrival of hundreds of Italian captives. After they had marched through the streets everyone turned their fury on the local Italian shopkeepers who owned the fish and chip shops and the ice-cream parlours. All their front windows were smashed to bits. My sister Nancy was injured by a brick that someone had thrown through the window of the little café where she worked during the weekends. When the prisoners of war eventually left for good some of my pals and I went up to have a look at Johnstone Castle. Inside, there were lots of little ornaments which had been carved by the prisoners before they left. All of them had been intricately handcrafted from lumps of black coal or pieces of wood that had been lying in or around the camp. On the damp walls there hung loads of beautiful paintings and sketches that had been copied by the bored foreign captives during their stay in Scotland. They were absolutely beautiful and I'll never forget them.

Every single boy in my class was football mad. We collected little cards with the faces of our favourite players on them which could then be put into a book when you had managed to collect the whole team, something which very few of us could afford to do. All these little cards were sold by the local newsagent who had opened a temporary establishment at the top of our street. I remember the owner of this shop once hatched a scheme which saw the sales of those football cards soar through the roof. To make sure that it was foolproof he even stamped the back of his cards with a special message thereby making certain that no other shop in the area would profit. He made it known that there was a prize up for grabs for the lucky boy who could gather the whole Glasgow Rangers Football Team in card-form. The prize was a beautiful leather football, which was proudly displayed in the window of his wee shop. Within days the news of that real leather football was sweeping every housing scheme and school in Johnstone. Hundreds of wee boys like myself had nightly dreams about kicking that "Real Leather and Hand-Stitched" football around the local public park. Weeks passed and everyone collected the cards at a furious pace. A nightmarish rumour was started when someone said that they knew of a posh boy with loads of money who had got his father to buy all the cards and had qualified to receive the ball. We all anxiously ran to the shop with our lungs bursting to see if this was true, but it plainly wasn't since the prize was still on view for everyone to see – and we slumped to the ground in relief. God only knows what we might have done to the posh kid if he had ever existed. It became apparent to us after about a month, however, that we all had one card missing from our collections, a player by the name of Eddie Rutherford. It wasn't long before we started to put two and two together and realise that we had all been the victims of a swindle by the wee newsagent. All sorts of thoughts ran through our minds. Someone suggested that one of us should divert the newsagent's attention while another grabbed the ball (it wouldn't be a crime, he'd asked for it hadn't he?) but in the long run we didn't have to resort to such desperate tactics since we found out that another local boy, who we didn't normally play with, actually had the much-sought-after card with Mr Rutherford's mug on it. Having to play with someone you didn't like was a small price to pay for claiming the ball, so it was immediately decided by the gang that I was the person who should go into the shop and claim it from the owner.

I duly strolled in and presented the wee newsagent with the cards. When he looked at the full set his teeth nearly fell out of his skinny mouth. He turned each card over and carefully examined the back of it for his special marking. Then he went into the back of the shop and put his glasses on and went through the whole examination procedure again and again. All the time that he was doing this I had to stand there watching the veins on the side of his neck stand out as he grew more angry and frustrated by the minute. Eventually, and reluctantly, he handed over the ball. I promptly grabbed it and ran like hell out of his shop. We took the new ball to the park and played football for the whole day, and even when it started to rain we still played on and on.

I told the boy who had given me the card about the reaction of the newsagent and went on to describe how carefully he had examined the back of all the cards, especially the Eddie Rutherford one. He laughed at my description but never said anything that afternoon. It was only later that I found out *he* had printed the special marking on the back of the card with one of those little home-printing sets that children used to get for Christmas. Well, as they say, necessity is the mother of invention . . . isn't it?

Sometimes we would find enough money for an outing to the pictures. Going to the local cinema, The George, at the end of the war was an experience not to be missed. For a start, the whole establishment was run by a funny wee man and a completely disorganised bunch of assistants. The usherettes were liable to murder you if you annoyed them, something which you dared not even consider since most of them were built like wrestlers. Occasionally some of us would muster up enough courage and attempt to sneak into the picture-house via the ramshackle toilets located towards the rear of the main hall. Their roofs were made out of old bits of corrugated-iron sheeting which made them look like something out of a South American shanty town. Anyone wanting to go had to squat or stand underneath them. It was also very, very dark, so it was little wonder that few people ventured out since they were liable to get a bigger fright from their visit than from the Boris Karloff flick that they had paid to see inside. But the toilets did provide the perfect illegal entrance for those of us who were fit, hard-up, bordering on the insane and who didn't object to getting their feet covered in whatever might be lying on the toilet floor.

Once inside, the entertainment was more often than not dished out by the antics of the audience than by the rotten films that invariably broke down at least three times in the course of an evening. There was one woman who sat down the very front of the hall who I will never forget. This individual must have weighed in near the fifteen-stone mark – in other words, she was one big lady. She was always to be found, night after night, sitting right down in the very front row, with various members of her family seated beside her. Indeed, there seemed to be a never-ending assortment and supply of young children that referred to her as their mother. At various points in the evening one of them would creep in from the back of the hall and ask in a loud voice what they should be making at home for their father's dinner when he returned from work. The fat mother would issue the instructions in an equally loud manner before returning to the much more pressing task of watching the screen. If the hero in the film, say Buster Crabbe as Buck Rogers or Olympic swimmer Johnny Weissmüller as Tarzan, was about to be lynched from behind by the villain of the piece, then the fat woman would scream out advice to him at the top of her voice. When she did this, all the people in the cinema would laugh and some of the small children would shout cat-calls at her. But I remember one night we all laughed at her. At the time she happened to be breast-feeding one of her many offspring, so she promptly heaved up one of her massive breasts and squirted us all, seated two rows behind. Needless to say we all kept our mouths shut in the future.

After a night's entertainment at the cinema we would walk home, following a route that led us by the town's Model lodging house for destitute men, which was at the end of McDowel Street. As the crowd of us walked by it we would break into a song:

> It's springtime in the Model,
> Down McDowel Street,
> The birds began to yodel and
> the mice began to squeak;
> "Get up you lazy bastards
> and wash your smelly feet!
> Because it's springtime in the
> Model down McDowel Street."

Inevitably, we also sang songs about Adolf Hitler; every town in the area had its own version of the following wee tune, but ours went like this:

> V for Victory, Dot Dot Dash,
> Hitler lost his wee moustache,
> When he funnit,
> He lost his bunnit,
> V for Victory, Dot Dot Dash!

After we had sung this about a hundred times in one night we would all arm ourselves with a pile of stones in readiness for the air-raid shelters that stood at the end of the main road. Some wag had expertly drawn the images of Hitler, Mussolini and Hirohito on them so, when we passed by, we all took part in a ritual bombardment of them with our stones. Many a night was spent knocking hell out of those air-raid shelters. I don't know if they ever got hit with real bombs or not but after we'd finished with them they certainly had an authentic look about them.

My recollections about the day that the war in Europe ended are somewhat hazy. I do remember that I was sitting in a class at school when our young teacher suddenly left the room. She returned five minutes later, her beautiful face streaming with tears, and told us that the war was over. Years later I found out that she had a young brother who had been kept prisoner in a POW camp in Italy. He was freed on the day that the war ended, which accounts for his sister's emotional reaction when she heard the good news.

I can vaguely recall the 1945 General Election. Everyone in the country got the shock of their lives when Churchill was turfed out of office by the small, bespectacled Clement Attlee, who was the Labour candidate. My father was a Labour supporter all his life so he was actually quite happy about the result. He never did forgive Churchill for putting the tanks in against the poor miners in the 1926 General Strike. As for me, the only real difference that I noticed was the fact that if you fell ill you were able to go to the doctor straight away without having to scrape the money together first. It was a unique period to live through I suppose, something that the historians call the "free teeth and glasses for everybody" era, but when you're young you don't really notice things like that. False teeth and glasses were still a few years away, thank God!

I moved into what is now called high school at the beginning of the 1950s. I never actually went very far to achieve this move since the secondary school was, in fact, part of the same three buildings that had housed my first school. Indeed, the chief distinction between the two places involved playgrounds. When I was younger I played my game of football in a small side playground, which was frequently raided by the older boys who slapped a few of our ears before stealing or bursting our precious football. When I got that little bit older, the roles were strangely reversed. I suddenly took a perverse delight in running through the small playground, clipping the wee boys around the ear before making off with their ball! The funny thing was that I had always sworn blind that I would never ever do such a thing. Still, I suppose that's human nature for you, eh?

My years at the Catholic secondary school were destined to be short-lived. I got into a fight at a bus-stop one night after school with one of the male teachers. He hauled me up in front of the head teacher the following day and eventually my mother and father also got dragged into the argument. To cut a long story short, I was asked to take my education elsewhere which meant moving to the local non-Catholic high school, Johnstone High. My younger sister, Dorothy, and younger brother, Alister, were also moved, although only Dorothy went to the same school as me. To be honest I hardly noticed any difference, except when we had to say prayers. During these times I was allowed to leave the room. The only antagonism that I can ever recall involved a stupid teacher who made the sign of the cross behind my back one morning, just as prayers were beginning and I was leaving. Apart from that, and the odd fight at the school gates,

I got along fine. I was helped by the fact that I was a good football player and I soon became a regular in the Johnstone High team. My sister Dorothy fitted in easily as well; in fact, she grew fond of the place in a way that I never did. For example, the local priest paid us a visit at home one night and asked her what she thought of her new school. She told him that she liked it and that there wasn't as much time wasted on saying prayers as there had been at our old place. When he heard that, the priest drew back his hand as if he was going to belt her one across the face. My brother Danny jumped to his feet and grabbed the priest's arm, telling him in no uncertain terms what he would do with him if he attempted to lay a hand on Dorothy. The priest was flung out the house by him and my father and, to the best of my knowledge, he never came back to visit us again. Every one of the family, however, still attended the chapel on a regular basis despite our apparent unorthodoxy.

I left Johnstone High School in September 1953, the day that I turned fifteen. The afternoon that I walked out I felt as though I could take the world on. There I was, strolling down the street, telling everybody that I had a new job to go to the following week with a local flax mill as a bank-boy. But I never stayed in this job very long, mainly because I injured my hand on one of the high-speed flax-machines that was housed within the factory. There was plenty of other work around the area though, so it wasn't long before a friend of mine, Frank Murney, was able to get me another job. I was to be a van-boy with a local "carrying" firm called Wilson Brothers for the next three years. I loved this job. We worked in a team of four or five on each van and I was soon subjected to every con trick in the book that the rest of the team tried out on new recruits. They dropped lit cigarettes into my brown overall pockets, they put raw fish into my sandwiches and they spiked my flask with every liquid known to man. Despite all these daily hazards, I grew to love the guys who I worked with. The job itself didn't give you much satisfaction but it did give you a couple of pounds in your pocket at the weekend. The money was important to me at that time since I was in my mid-teens and just starting to realise that life held all sorts of possibilities. The hair was now combed in the popular "Tony Curtis" style, the trousers had to be exactly sixteen inches wide and the music we listened to was labelled "Rock and Roll" by an American DJ called Alan Freed.

Johnstone in the mid-1950s wasn't exactly world-famous for its entertainment facilities. At home the family spent its nights listening to the radio. We all sat in silence allowing our minds to wander, whether it be along the paths that Dick Barton, Special Agent, trod, or through the mysteries of the *The Man in Black*, which sent us all up to bed with our teeth chattering. Our weekends consisted mainly of walking up and down the High Street. If it was raining, we would go to an Italian café in nearby Kilbarchan owned by wee Louis. The interior was painted in the cheap, gaudy colours that were really popular back then. We would hang our coats up and sit in one of the stalls located around the walls and order a bowl of hot peas and vinegar. The greasy food being cooked made all the windows steam up on the inside, causing them to run with rivers of condensation. We would try and make the peas last as long as possible so that we wouldn't have to go back outside into the elements. I remember one night in particular three pals and I sat inside eating hot peas for hours. In fact, we sat so long that we all began to fart loudly, much to wee Louis' disgust. He banned us all for a week. We tried to explain to him that it was *his* peas that were the cause of the offensive noise but he wouldn't have any of it.

If we had any money we would occasionally head for Paisley Town Hall on a Sunday night when it held the "go as you please" concerts. This allowed every would-be rock-and-roll vocalist within a ten-mile radius (who had been secretly miming to Guy Mitchell's "She Wears Red Feathers" in front of the wardrobe mirror for a fortnight) to get up on stage and attempt to strut his stuff. Needless to say it was more of a laugh than anything else. In fact, what I most clearly remember is the amount of stringless guitars that suddenly appeared. Every potential Presley, you see, knew that his image was fatally incomplete unless he had a guitar slung around his neck with which he could strike the appropriate poses during the songs. It also provided him with an excellent weapon in the event of the crowd laughing too much or if an angry boyfriend should try to lynch him after a successful groin-thrust encore. The reason for the lack of strings on them was simply because very few of the performers, if any at all, could actually play the guitar properly, so most of them just sang their hearts out while they *slapped* the guitar in time to the rhythm. No wonder we never went there very often.

The local Drill Hall was the meeting place for the army cadets. I went there one night, more out of desperation and boredom than anything else, to see what it was like. Joining the army had been at the back of my mind for years. Perhaps it was all those American war films that I'd seen, I don't know, but the idea certainly appealed to me. Men in uniform all seemed to speak in clandestine terms, casually referring to "manoeuvres", "map-reading", "reconnaissance" and "sharp-shooting". These phrases suggested heroic adventures in far-flung tropical locations, with exotic sun-kissed beauties tagging along for mere decorative purposes. Small wonder that I soon became one of the cadets' most enthusiastic members.

Queen Elizabeth visited Paisley in 1953 and the Army Cadet Force were asked to organise the crown control. I was really excited the night before her visit and I sat polishing my cap-badge and brass belt-buckle well into the early hours. Next morning crowds from all over the area converged on the town when the Queen was due to arrive. It was an extremely hot summer's day so us cadets were kept busy with members of the crowd who had fainted after being overcome with a combination of heat, fat female feet squeezed into tight wee shoes and too much lukewarm Irn Bru.

After our company had saluted the Queen as she passed by, we moved on to a memorial service which was being held in the local Kelburn cinema. The film that was playing was called *Standing Room Only*, an appropriate title given the fact that everyone and his brother had piled into the small building. At the end of the service a very tall, striking figure suddenly strolled on to the stage. Everyone stopped talking and looked towards him. I gazed in awe at the immaculately-pressed military outfit that he was wearing. The jacket was made of lightweight linen for tropical conditions and was a biscuit-brown colour. Along the left-hand side of his chest hung a row of gleaming medals that sparkled when the light hit them. He looked totally restrained, calm, yet very much quietly in command of the situation. I noted his every precise movement from the back of the hall where I stood wearing my heavy, sweaty and itchy battledress. For a second there was silence while everyone took a private moment to digest the size and presence of this soldier. Initially, none of us cadets knew who he was but, after he started to speak, a whisper passed down the line. Someone told me that his name was General Colin "Tiny" Barber, reputedly the tallest serving officer in any of the three services. I kept staring at his outfit; the sharply-pressed trousers, the made-to-measure jacket, the perfectly-knotted tie, his shining shoes and that wide row of medals. I visualised myself wearing the same outfit, leading the same, dignified, military life and commanding the same kind of respect. From that moment on, I knew that my days as a "weekend warrior" with the local cadet force were numbered. I wanted to be a real soldier.

One afternoon when I was out in the Wilson Brothers van in Glasgow, I told the driver that I was taking a long lunch-hour. Within ten minutes I had made my way around to the Royal Engineer's recruiting centre in the city's Bath Street. A large sergeant sat behind the desk inside and I asked him how quickly I could join if I signed all the forms that very afternoon. He asked me some details then told me that, given the fact that I was almost eighteen years old, I would be given call-up papers for National Service any day. "Why don't you wait till then?" he suggested. I told him that I wanted to go as soon as possible, so he said that he would rush the application through for me. So I signed up for no less than twenty-two years with an option to leave at the end of three. He congratulated me on my wise decision and said that I would be better treated and entitled to more privileges than the National Servicemen whom I was sure to bump into in the future. So, after all these reassuring words, I left the building feeling quite pleased with myself; I was my own man and I was, at last, in full control of my own life. But when my medical forms arrived at the house a few days later, all hell broke loose since I hadn't summoned up the guts to tell anyone in the family about my imminent military manoeuvres. I stuck to my imaginary guns though and, despite my parents' objections, finally left Johnstone to join the army two weeks later.

The night I left the town, I was feeling miserable so I headed for the "Celtic Bar", an infamous local hard-drinking den, where I fortified myself with just enough liquid to put a grin on my face. I tried to look as brave as possible when my sister, Nancy, and a girl that I was dating at the time waved me off on the train to Glasgow. The short journey into the city flew by and as the alcohol took effect I began to enjoy the unique feeling of youthful independence which even winter weather couldn't destroy.

Apart from a brief foray to Wembley to see a Scotland and England football match, I had never been out of Scotland in my life so, in theory, I should have been a little bit apprehensive when, on 5 November 1958, I boarded the 9.15 Glasgow to Worcester train. But I wasn't apprehensive, because when you're a good-looking eighteen-year-old, sporting a greased-back head of hair, with your itchy-feet firmly planted inside blue-suede brothel-creepers and you're full of drink, you start to believe that you really can take on the world . . . and win!

Chapter Two

THE MILES DISAPPEARED as the soothing effects of the previous night's drinking slowly, but comfortably, slipped away. The journey to Worcester was shortened after I met another army recruit on the train, Bobby Campbell. We both did our best to convince each other that we weren't nervous, but I think the bravado never really worked since the excitement kept us both awake throughout the eight-hour journey.

The weather in Worcester was, unfortunately, just as bad as anything that we had left behind in Glasgow. Bobby and I stood on the station platform for five minutes with numb fingers wrapped around the freezing handles of our small cases and rubbed our bleary eyes. I think we expected something momentous to happen at any moment but, alas, there was no welcoming committee from the Royal Engineers. We set off up the road towards the army camp after obtaining some directions from a local lady who was taking her little dog for an early morning walk. The wind whistled around us so I eventually gave up trying to light a cigarette under the lapel of my jacket. A slow, steady drizzle had settled in as we approached the rows of wooden barracks which were painted in a dodgy shade of brown. We walked through the high gates and looked around for someone to acknowledge our arrival from foreign parts. The only person I could see was a barrel-chested man who was striding purposely across what looked like a wee carpark. I lit up another smoke and shouted over to him:

"Hey Jimmy! It's us, we're here, by the way!"

He stopped dead in his tracks. I stubbed out my fag and confidently headed over towards him. I began my speech while he eyed me up and down. He slowly took in the hair, the suit, the "Slim-Jim" tie, the turn-ups and finally, worst of all, the immaculate blue-suede brothel-creepers. Suddenly he started to shout at me while his face turned a weird shade of red and his mouth twisted and contorted itself firing out unintelligible phrases in a strange English accent. I just gaped at him in surprise as he jabbed a flabby finger in the direction of my shoes. I was soon to learn that this man was the Regimental Sergeant-Major and, under his law, we had stepped on to his "Holy-ground" (the parade ground), wearing distinctly unmilitary footwear! He ordered me to remove the offending shoes. I did what I was told and handed them to him, – "Perhaps he was wanting to go up the dancing that night," I thought to myself. But he grabbed the good shoes and threw them away. I was shocked. Not only did this man have a terrible English accent but he also clearly had no taste in quality footwear. Then he made me march up and down the parade ground in my stockinged feet for ten minutes or more. After I'd finished I was told my hair was far too long, so next stop was the barbers. Deciding to take no chances, I instructed the barber to, in my estimation, take "a good bit off of it". But what I regarded as "a good bit" and what the Regimental Sergeant-Major thought was "a good bit" were totally different. I made a grand total of three visits to the barber on that first morning before he was happy with the length of my hair, which as far as I could see had completely ceased to exist. Indeed, if you look at my picture taken later the same morning you'll see a shell-shocked, well-shorn and slightly light-headed young man staring back at you through pleading eyes. I was already starting to question my sanity.

Breakfast consisted of a plate of porridge which had been steeped overnight in sugar, ensuring the milk that I poured on never had a cat in hell's chance of soaking in. This was followed by a fried egg (that hadn't seen a hen for years) slapped between two slices of week-old bread. I gazed down at the food silently, before moving away from the counter. Suddenly a Scottish voice shouted at me:

"Oi, Jock, you forgot this," he cried, holding up a tea-mug.

As I took it I recognised the face of Dinny Hasson, an old school pal from Johnstone. It was like meeting your best friend in the desert, I could have kissed him. He asked me a few questions and said he'd see me later on when he'd more time. I waved and grinned as I moved away. The tea tasted funny since it was laced with bromide, a questionable potion of sorts which was supposed to curtail any sexual ambitions that the more rampant new recruits might have had. But they needn't have bothered. The porridge and greasy eggs had already put most of us out of commission in that department . . . .

Then we were issued with our kit from stores. We lined up and shouted out our height and other details to the soldiers who were in charge of equipment. I'm sure they ignored us half the time and just flung out whatever was near to hand. Amid cries from various wee recruits about the size of the trousers that they had been landed with, we shuffled with the large pile of clothes towards our new homes. I stared in amazement at the vests; those things had more hair on them than the billet's carpets! The rest of the underwear was just as bad, the long-johns, for example, had a gusset on them that reached down to my knees. Still, I assumed they would all come in handy if we were ever posted to fight out on the Russian Front in Siberia.

My bed in the billet was positioned adjacent to an old-fashioned "pot-bellied" stove and I used everything under the sun as fuel for it. In my first few days I regularly nodded asleep next to its comforting warmth which probably reminded me of our coal fire back home. New recruits were warned about pilferers so all my prize possessions were planked under my mattress. Once I accidentally fell asleep halfway through writing a letter home and I awoke to find my little book of stamps had been stolen. I quietly looked around and discovered them on top of a locker belonging to the guy across the room from me. When I claimed them, he was lying under the covers of his bed taking an afternoon nap. I challenged him loudly to explain the apparent theft. He slowly roused from his slumbers. As he came out from under the covers I began to shake. This guy was bloody massive! He looked down at me and asked me to repeat what I'd said. By this time everybody in the place was listening, so I took the bull by the balls and told him in no uncertain terms "not to mess with my stamps again". He looked around at the crowd, hesitated for a moment, then apologised. I think it was the Scottish accent which did the trick – I was only five foot six inches but I felt like King Kong.

The next few days saw us all being marched to death but, given my previous experience in the local cadets, the shock wasn't as great for me as it might have been. It was hilarious watching some of the other new boys trying to march properly though, for if the bloke in front went wrong then the whole lot went with him. We must have marched up and down that parade-ground at least a thousand times during our first week in Worcester.

Within the next few days we were given our army number. The issuing sergeant darkly informed us about the treacherous consequences that could mysteriously befall us should we ever forget what our number was. Many a young recruit, he claimed, had disappeared during the night in suspicious circumstances because he'd failed to recite his number on parade . . . backwards! My number was 23494533. I worked out a system which helped me to remember it easily. The whole formula was based on the number nine. This was how I did it. Take the first four digits, 2349; you add the first three, $2+3+4$, then it equals the fourth, 9. The sum of the next two digits, 4 and 5, equalled the third, which was also 9, as was the sum of the last two figures (ie, $3\times3=9$). It sounds complicated now but at the time it was a godsend and I was soon able to recite the number backwards to the sergeant who was desperate to catch anyone out.

The mail we received was distributed on parade by a horrible little corporal who took a perverted delight in throwing everyone's letters on to the ground. This practice continued even in the worst of weathers, so our envelopes were often soggy when we picked them up. One day the little corporal came to a letter that was addressed to a guy by the name of Bowles. He shouted out the name and Mr Bowles went up and collected his letter but, instead of opening it, he simply glanced at the writing then threw it into a large puddle. The corporal did a little dance with rage and demanded an explanation.

"What's your name, soldier?" he screamed.

The big guy looked at him for a moment, then told him in a heavy Aberdonian accent. But the diminutive corporal completely lost his temper since he thought the reply had been "Balls". He marched the guy off and took him up in front of another officer. Eventually Mr Bowles was let off, although he was warned to open his mouth wider when asked his name in the future.

Worcester was really only an initiation camp and we were stationed there for no more than three weeks. All the new recruits were pushed to their physical limits at least once a day in order to make us as fit as possible. I hated the ten-mile runs and I was convinced they did us more harm than good. On one occasion in particular I ran until I thought my chest was about to explode. I barely made it back to the billet in one piece before heading off to the toilets where I was sure I was going to throw up. I entered the darkened building and made my way to the first empty cubicle. The baggy shorts were hauled down and I sat on the toilet with my sore head in my sweaty hands. I felt really light-headed but chanced sitting back so I might take in a deep breath. When I sat back the top of my head suddenly touched something hard. I fumbled around and eventually stood up to look at what was obstructing me. There, halfway up the toilet wall, was a young man, hanging by the neck. His eyes were bloated like two red snooker-balls and all his limbs swung vacantly. He was clearly dead. I grabbed my drawers up around my waist and, believe it or not, managed to find enough strength to run for an officer. After explaining what had happened I was thanked and told to go for a mug of sweet tea which would help to calm me down. The cook who gave me the tea asked me why I looked so shocked, so I slowly recounted my gory tale to him. After I'd finished he calmly kept on chewing his gum and continued to wipe off the catering equipment:

"Well," he drawled, "we get a couple of them with every fresh crop." He stopped cleaning and grinned over at me as I lifted the cup to my mouth with trembling hands. "I wonder who's going to be next?" he said quietly.

As you can imagine, it was hard being away from home for the first time. The only way to survive was to try and make some friends. I became good pals with another young soldier, Glyndoor John Morris, from Pontyprith in Wales. He was a real gentle giant who never smoked or drank and was a champion swimmer and weightlifter. Since it was too far and too expensive for me to travel back to Scotland over the festive period, I ended up spending Christmas with Glynn and his family. It was a unique experience and one that I'll always remember fondly.

Our next place of residence was in No 3 Barracks in Farnborough. After Worcester it was like going out of the frying-pan and into the fire. It was a real hell-hole altogether where the army tried to make you or break you, there was no middle ground. The watchword was supposed to be "discipline" but I soon discovered that what they really meant was obedience. In other words, we had to obey every ludicrous order that was thrown at us, no matter how stupid it might appear to be.

We received our rifles at Farnborough and were told that they were our "best friends". Our weapons were the "303"s which gave you a sore shoulder after you'd fired them if you happened to hold them incorrectly. I had managed to gain some marksmanship experience in the cadets so I enjoyed visiting the rifle-range. Inevitably I passed my marksmanship tests easily, so the corporal assigned me to "mark-up" the targets with a pointer for the rest of the corps. I soon saw this job as a means to a financial end since loads of the soldiers were desperate to pass the exam and willingly paid me money to punch a few holes in the target for them. Many a soldier appeared to hit a bull's-eye when in fact he'd probably hit a couple of cows in a nearby field.

If you dropped that rifle on parade then you would be dressed in full uniform, your FFSMOK (Full Field Service Marching Order Kit) and forced to run around the parade ground holding the heavy weapon above your head until you dropped with exhaustion. If that didn't break you, then you would be escorted into the ablutions, the washing area, where all the hot showers and baths would be turned on. After the place had filled up with scalding steam, you would be forced to do lung-bursting cardiovascular exercises, still wearing all the gear. I was punished in this fashion until the sweat poured from me and soaked right through all the layers that I was wearing. It looked as if I had been thrown into a river wearing full kit.

Our marching-boots were another case in point. Their toes were covered in little dimples which had to be removed before we would get a really good shine on them. To remove the dimples you had to heat the end of a spoon until it was red hot, then burn them off, one by one. It took two or three hours of elbow grease to achieve a decent shine on the boot. Nowadays they have boots that are ready for shining the moment you receive them but it was different then and many a weekend was spent beside a tin of boot-polish instead of beside a local bar.

I slowly began to take a real pride in my kit which had to be laid out every morning for inspection. Everything had to be measured out exactly, underpants four inches, socks two inches, and I ran around the bed with a wee ruler checking everything twice. Even my drinking mug suddenly became very important. If that mug had even the slightest mark inside its rim, it would be smashed on the parade ground. Over a period of time the amount of bromide mixed into our tea meant the mugs developed a brown coating which was difficult to remove. My mug was relatively clean in comparison with others but I still went through about ten or eleven during my stay at Farnborough. Every time that I appeared on parade with my mug swinging by my side, I would be stopped by this one particularly evil corporal and forced to recheck inside the rim. He always, without exception, found something wrong with it – before he smashed it to bits in front of me. I had to pay for it to be replaced. To this day I'm sure there was a degree of method in this apparent madness. I've always believed, you see, the Ministry of War had thousands of mugs left over after the Second World War which they knew they would have to get rid of in one way or another; so, having the corporals introduce and enforce this stupid rule, then having all soldiers *pay* for the mugs to be replaced, ensured that they recouped at least some of their expenses.

The training at Farnborough was really horrendous and at night you could hear grown men crying, wanting to go home to their mothers. Others had more guts and they used to get down on their knees by the side of their beds and say their prayers. I often wished I had the same courage of my conviction but I could never say my prayers in such a public fashion. After the lights were out and everyone else was asleep, I would turn my head to the wall, close my eyes tightly and then say my prayers to myself. I knew that somebody, somewhere, was listening.

Some of the really desperate characters, who decided enough was enough, jumped the wall and deserted. The next time you saw them they were in the "glass-house", where the prisoners were kept. They stuck out like sore-thumbs because of the skin-head haircuts they were given as part of their punishment. The corporals took a real pleasure in degrading and humiliating the men and trying to find all the weak points in our different characters. When they wanted to annoy me, for example, they would call me a "Glasgow corner-boy" when I was out on parade with all the other men. That really upset me since I was never a "corner-boy" in any sense of the word. It got to the point where I began to fantasise about sneaking out of my bed at night, making my way over to their tents and slitting all their throats while they lay asleep. But I never considered running back home since I knew my father would have kicked my backside for being a coward and then put me on the first train back.

One guy lived only thirty miles from the barracks, so he arranged for his mother to visit him regularly with food parcels which were filled to the brim with goodies. We called him "Mouser" because he used to wake up late at night, reach under his blankets with a torch and carefully unwrap his mother's parcels. We could all hear him as he got stuck into the chocolates and cakes, delicacies which many of us hadn't even seen before, never mind eaten. Eventually we ran out of patience, however, mostly because he never shared anything but also because his nocturnal feasts kept the rest of us awake, so we decided to teach him a lesson. I volunteered to loosen the bolts on his bed during the day, so that by the time he started fumbling around for his secret parcel the whole bed was on the point of falling apart. The entire structure collapsed around him just as he was taking a mouthful of something nice. As he struggled to maintain his dignity amid a sea of scones and pillows some other bugger cracked open a stink-bomb on top of him. Poor old Mouser was never the same again.

The day training finished we all lined up in our barracks and stood to attention as two corporals inspected us. But instead of the usual routine, they just strolled in and told us to relax. I thought I had misheard the command, so I kept standing. One of them strolled over to me and grinned:

"Relax McGinley," he said, "your training's finished, you're one of us now, a regular."

He offered me a cigarette and asked me some questions about my fondness for the army football team I played for. I looked at him out of the corner of my eye. I grabbed for the cigarette, thanked him for it, but never budged an inch. "There had to be a catch, they must be trying to pull a flanker on us on our very last day," I thought silently to myself.

"I told you to stand at ease, McGinley," repeated the corporal. "It's over."

I chanced a smile. Nothing happened. I asked him for permission to smoke the cigarette that he'd given me. He laughed and told me to smoke away. Suddenly the other corporal pulled out a massive, deadly-looking bayonet. He held it up in front of us. No one dared say a word. He lifted his arm up in a wide arc and, with all his strength, flung the bayonet into the highly polished floor. It embedded itself deeply into the surface:

"There you go, boys," he laughed. "That's for the next lot of raw recruits to clean up when they arrive next week."

My next posting was to Ripon in Yorkshire, where I did a plant operator's course. It was a good course which saw me becoming very efficient in the operation of bulldozers and other heavy equipment. Apart from the practical work, we were also required to participate in lectures which dealt with the theory and design of various types and models of engines. By the end of it I felt as if I had learned something really worthwhile. The nightlife in Ripon was pretty good as well. We went to local cafés and the dancing on a regular basis so we were never short of company.

One Saturday morning some friends and I volunteered to go grouse-beating for the posh people who lived nearby. The deal was that we would get the previous Friday night off if we turned out at six o'clock the next morning, so we thought that there was nothing to it. We reported bright and early for breakfast and afterwards were given two gigantic "doorstep" slices of bread and a lump of cheese to see us through the whole day. This was our "packed-lunch", we were told. We went out on to the moors with other beaters after being told to hit the undergrowth with a stick whilst making as much noise as was humanly possible. And as we made complete fools of ourselves, the local gentry, dressed in their tweed-outfits and sipping from silver hip-flasks, took pot-shots at our feathered friends who periodically made doomed bids for freedom.

After everyone tired of playing with their guns we were invited back to a small gathering which was to be held in some landowner's large front garden. My Liverpool friend and I managed to con a cup of tea out of somebody, which we drank whilst keeping an appropriate distance from the real guests. It was a cold and chilly morning so we wanted to get back to the billet as soon as possible and we certainly didn't have any time for small-talk and local gossip. But I suddenly noticed a strangely familiar figure standing amongst the group to my right-hand side. His face rang a bell and I was walking towards him before I realised it.

"Excuse me, sir," I stammered, "but are you General Sir Colin 'Tiny' Barber?"

"Yes," he replied. "And who might you be, laddie?"

"McGinley, sir," I answered, as I saluted him. "I saw you when I was a cadet, the day the Queen visited Paisley, sir."

He looked down his nose at me for what seemed an eternity. I was sure he would have me thrown out. Then he smiled slowly.

"I remember the day well," he said.

He snapped his fingers and a little effeminate butler appeared from nowhere.

"Arrange for this man and his friends to come over for tea at my house one night when it's suitable for them," barked the general to the little man. Then he turned to me. "Is that all right with you, McGinley?"

"Oh fine, sir," I grinned.

I saluted him about twenty times as I retreated towards my friends. We left quickly and headed back towards the billet. I was floating on air.

"You are off your nut," said my scouse pal when I told him about our invitation. "We shouldn't talk to the likes of him. We're dead."

I never followed through the invitation though. On the night I was due to go to tea with General Sir Colin "Tiny" Barber I was languishing in the billet after being confined to barracks for twenty-eight consecutive days. What really annoys me is that for the life of me I still can't remember what I was being punished for.

Then, out of the blue, the whole corps were notified that they were to be posted abroad. I was told my posting was to be in Osnabruk in West Germany. Where?

We left Ripon early one morning a week later, bound for Southampton. It was 27 May 1957 when the ship left the port and sailed east for Germany via the Hook of Holland. The journey was excellent, it was the very first time that I had ever gone such a long distance on a ship and I was pleased with my ability to keep my dinner down. Many of my fellow Royal Engineers weren't so lucky – some of them spent the entire journey looking down the bowl of a toilet or gazing into the choppy sea.

When we eventually arrived in Germany, the first thing that caught my attention was the cleanliness of the countryside and the towns. Even the German railway stations and their staff seemed to be a lot tidier than the usual lot who inhabited Glasgow Central Station.

Our new camp was housed inside the local ex-Nazi headquarters. When you walked through the gates there were two four-storey buildings facing you, made of dark red bricks and very imposing the first time you saw them. The cook-house was on the left, and the low buildings to the right made up the guard buildings with the parade ground further down. I was allocated to share a room with three other chaps and my duties were mainly involved with looking after the stores which were filled with sports equipment.

Initially the social life in Germany was rather strange for us and we didn't help matters with our lop-sided belief that the problem lay with the natives, who we classed as the "bloody foreigners". Indeed, we used to get quite peeved because the locals couldn't speak any English, never mind understand our Scottish accents. After an abortive trip to the German cinema we ended up becoming regulars at the British forces cinema where at least we could understand the film's plot. However, the German beer was wonderful and I spent night after night stuffing myself with these strange things called "pretzels" which I used to dip, much to the barman's apparent disgust, into a bowl of strong German mustard.

Generally the local people were very nice to soldiers but we were warned by our commanding officers always to be on our guard against any trouble-makers in the younger set. The scrapes that we did get into were, more often than not, of our own doing. One night, for example, I downed a deadly amount of drink (usually a combination of beer and a local drink that could have run a car), which caused my head to spin. I sat down on the edge of the kerb and carefully placed my throbbing head into my hands. Then a lovely woman appeared and in faltering English asked me if I needed any help. I presume I told her I did because she subsequently accompanied me back to the barracks. When we reached the gate the guards went crazy. They shouted at her and, despite her assurances that everything was above board, flung me into the pokey to dry out. I was confined to quarters for seven days for procuring the services of a prostitute! Her reputation by all accounts was well known to everyone except me. In fact, our whole corps was extraordinarily innocent when it came to the whole subject of sex. On arrival in Germany I couldn't have told you what a "red-light" area was and, despite my blue-suede brothel-creepers, I hadn't the slightest idea about houses of ill-repute. We certainly didn't have too many of them back home in Johnstone. The very first night that we visited the red-light area illustrates just how green we really were. All the girls that were plying their trade stood behind full-length windows wearing little outfits that left nothing to the imagination. When all of us strolled by with our eyes popping out of our heads they immediately saw their financial boats coming in, so they started waving and beckoning us to move closer to their windows. We decided to chance no more than a quick glance at what was on offer before touring the rest of the town. Everyone agreed later on the reason why they picked us out of the evening crowds to wave at – we were simply the best looking soldiers that had passed through the area in a long time. I mean, what other explanation could there possibly be for them enthusiastically trying to attract our attention?

The summers that I spent in Germany were wonderful. The Rhine flowed right behind the barracks where we were stationed, so we used to get all our swimming togs together, pack some food and head off for the banks of that magnificent, swollen river. There, with a few local German girls in tow, we'd sit all day long watching Germans dive off the side of the numerous high bridges that were dotted every couple of miles along the river.

After Osnabruk, the whole corps was sent on manoeuvres to Hamlin which, of course, is known the world over for the legend of its "Pied Piper". We spent most of our time building bailey-bridges in remote locations so our accommodation was always under canvas. The town of Hamlin is beautiful. All the streets are covered in ancient cobble-stones and the medieval architecture is visible on every street. It was a real honour to march through that town although I did have a bad accident in it one Saturday night. On that particular night I missed the tram-car back to the barracks so myself and a couple of friends began the long trek back. As we walked along the road we suddenly realised that we were being followed by a group of German youths on motorbikes. I tried to run away from them but they easily caught up with me and chased me on to the pavement. I slipped on the wet surface and one of the motorbikes ran right over the top of my outstretched legs. As I lay there screaming in agony, a German policeman stood over me and pointed his handgun at my head. He seemed to think I was a drunken German but soon helped me when he realised I was a serviceman who was in genuine pain. He arranged for an ambulance to take me to the hospital so that I could have my burst knee-caps attended to. Within a few days I was, thankfully, on my feet again and they soon had me doing light-duties in and around the barracks.

Lots of the soldiers stationed in Germany in the 1950s became involved with the blackmarket in one way or another and I was no exception. A local barman was desperate to get his hands on petrol so I used to organise the odd few gallons for him from time to time. In return he would allow me to eat and drink anything I wanted. One night I got really drunk on his strong German beer and barely made it back to the barracks in one piece. The corporal bawled me out for my drunken antics and told me I was in no fit state to go out on the corps' radio manoeuvres which were taking place that evening. I lay down on the bed and fell asleep within two minutes.

Another soldier was drafted in to replace me in the one-ton radio truck. He was killed in a crash, along with three other young soldiers, when the driver attempted to overtake another vehicle as it rounded a sharp bend in the road. The driver suffered a broken-neck and was the only survivor of the crash. He was later found to be negligent over the incident and was sentenced to some time in military prison. One of the young men who was tragically killed in the crash was a friend of mine called Peter. He spoke with a polite, upper-class accent and came from the south-west of England. He used to rib me about my accent and I joked with him about his; we were like chalk and cheese but we got on like a house on fire. I quietly respected his abilities as a radio-operator and was often shamed by his unfailing generosity when I was hard up. He was a real friend.

All the belongings of the deceased were brought back to the camp later that night. I was on duty in the store-room when the pile of clothes was unceremoniously dumped on the bare concrete floor. A big bastard of a corporal pounced on Peter's clothes:

"There's a cap-badge missing here," he sneered. "I want this man charged for the cap-badge – dead or not, someone pays when army property goes missing."

I blew my top and hit the corporal twice before being dragged away. Our officer decided not to charge me over the incident but I was prevented from going to Peter's funeral because they were frightened I might say something to his parents about the corporal's remarks. It was a terrible experience to endure when I was only nineteen years old; the confusion was intensified by the fact that I had previously always trusted my superior officers and it took me a while to come to terms with the callous attitude some of them had when it came to human lives.

A "Displaced-Persons" camp was located near our barracks. If we had extra food, spare blankets or some cigarettes we would take them up to the camp and pass them through the wire to the people inside. I thought it was similar to the POW camp which I'd often visited as a boy in Scotland but, after I'd visited it a few times, I came to realise that this camp was full of survivors of the Nazi Holocaust. I was young and had little or no real idea of what these poor wretches had experienced so I decided to make a trip to the infamous Belsen extermination camp whilst I was in Germany. When we arrived at the gates of the camp we weren't sure what to do. Why were we here? Were we tourists looking at a notable landmark? We couldn't put our finger on it but the whole trip was beginning to look like a bad idea. A few German guides solemnly led other visitors by us, through the gates and into the camp itself. We just stood there; the heavy overpowering sun beat down on me but despite this oppressive heat I still felt as cold as ice. "I'm not going in," I whispered to my friend. He nodded silently and we left. Belsen had seen enough visitors in the past.

An Asian flu-virus swept through the camp and, since I was still weak after my encounter with the motorbike, I was one of the first to fall ill. I was placed in a makeshift hospital for a few days while the worst of the fever passed, then told that I was due to be sent back to the UK before being posted abroad. I departed from Germany on 14 October 1957 and travelled for some twenty-four hours before I reached Ripon. I was so ill with the virus that I still cannot recall the journey nor what mode of transport was used to shift me. I was in Catterick hospital in England for a few nights then I was allowed to return to the barracks in Ripon. The whole corps was uncertain about our posting abroad – at that stage no one knew where they were being sent. I wasn't even thinking about going aboard at that time since I was already packing for my three weeks' embarkation leave which I'd decided to spend at home in Scotland.

I arrived home and was duly fussed over by the family who were all eager to hear my tales about life in the army. The only member of the family who had an axe to grind was my brother, Davie, who had just arrived home from doing his national service in Kenya. Davie had encountered regular soldiers during his national service and decided that they all came from borstals, prison, broken homes or families, or were simply social misfits in one way or another. He was a bit ashamed that he had a brother (me!) who was a regular and thought that I had unintentionally brought disgrace on the family. The moment he saw me he swung a punch and started to wrestle with me on the ground in a way that only real brothers can understand. We eventually made up and settled our differences and I soon realised that Davie was more worried and concerned about me than anything else. Punching was his painful way of displaying his affection for his wee brother.

As soon as I'd enough time I headed for my wee pal, Frank Murney, who had already been called up for service. Frank and I had been pals since school and the pair of us had worked together at Wilson Brothers. We met and swapped stores about the army, although mine were a bit more enthusiastic than Frank's since he hated it and couldn't wait to be done with the whole thing. The pair of us went out for the night to a local café which served excellent tea and had a first-rate selection of Presley records on its juke-box.

As we entered the café we noticed two young girls sitting in the corner of the room. Both girls were striking looking in different ways; one had lovely blonde curly hair whilst the smaller, younger one, had beautiful long, black hair. Frank and I were joined by a few other locals and we all watched the two girls from a distance as we sipped our tea. One of them bet me ten shillings that I couldn't see the smaller dark-haired girl home for the evening. I strolled over and asked her. She didn't say "yes" or "no" but I wasn't caring. I followed her anyway just to make sure I got the ten shillings. As we walked along the road she told me her name was Alice and that she was only fourteen years old. Over the next few days I turned up at the school-gates wearing my uniform – which proved to be something of a talking-point among her giggling pals – wanting to walk her home. We eventually parted the night before I was due to go back to England. At the time, I wasn't too optimistic about our future together, mainly because she wasn't a Roman Catholic, but I was quietly pleased when she said she would write to me when I'd gone back to the army.

Frank, meanwhile, was in a state of confusion about his military future. He hadn't a clue about where his next posting was going to be. I asked him if he'd received any news.

"Osnabruk in Germany with the 38 Engineer Corps," replied Frank.

"It can't be," I retorted. "I'm in that corps and we're due at Ripon to be posted abroad next week."

It was then that it dawned on us that there was a good chance we would be posted abroad together. I had been on standby for a few days in case the situation in Northern Ireland deteriorated any further but word reached me saying I was to be sent to an island in the Pacific instead. Frank received similar instructions. Frank and I had played together as children, we'd gone to school together, we'd started our first jobs together and now we were going to be posted abroad together. It was almost too good to be true.

It was a day or two before Christmas 1957 when Frank and I left Johnstone and headed down to Ripon. One of the first things we had to do upon arrival at the barracks was to attend a film show. Everyone who was posted abroad was required to watch this little untitled film before leaving the country. Frank and myself had heard a few vague and somewhat garbled rumours about its contents beforehand but none of them seemed to make much sense to us so we were more or less in the dark about the whole thing as we settled in our seats. I had a sneaking suspicion that we might be shown a film about the foreign beauty-spots where we would be posted. But, instead of waterfalls, sand, palm-trees and sun-drenched coastlines, the projector stuttered into life with a cartoon! Now we all knew we weren't exactly intellectuals but we presumed we were beyond the Disney stage. A little animated dark-skinned lady wearing a grass-skirt entered the frame from the right-hand side, some Hawaiian music accompanying her as she swayed provocatively to and fro. We all laughed on cue. Frank folded his arms and muttered something about "This is dead good, eh?" then the wee woman introduced us to her beach-hut and winked sexily at a soldier who had entered the frame on the left. She gestured to the soldier by lifting up her skirt and pointed to the little hut but he refused to enter. The exotic beauty wasn't to be thwarted, however, and she winked and swayed till the wee soldier could take no more. As his lust got the better of him and he finally flung caution to the wind and entered the hut, we all cheered and clapped and shouted advice. The next image that flashed on to the screen stunned us all into a shocked silence. A man lay on top of a hospital operating-table with his manhood (which was in a hell of a state) dangling for all the world to see. The narrator had an Orson Welles-like voice which boomed out in suitably apocalyptic tones:

"THIS SOLDIER HAS VENEREAL DISEASE!!"

Neither Frank nor I had a clue what this dreadful condition was. I nudged my wee pal and asked him if he knew what our "venereal" was and enquired into the method by which it caught a "disease". Before he could offer an answer the film showed a close-up of the patient's scab-infested and pus-ridden appendage, in glorious technicolor.

I recoiled in horror as wee Frank stared at his crotch in speechless amazement. All around me grown men were requesting permission to leave the room just as the film showed a gigantic needle-like instrument being inserted into the poor guy's willie. Once inside it unfolded and expanded like a little cocktail-umbrella, then the patient screamed in mortal agony as the lethal device was pulled out. The unfortunate wretch eventually passed-out completely, along with half the audience, when the process was finally over.

"Jesus, Frank, what did you think of that?" I spluttered after the film stopped running.

"I'm not going near any wee huts, no way, no wee huts . . ." gibbered a shaking Frank as we left the room.

The cold weather had begun to set in just as we arrived back at Ripon. One of my duties was to deliver coal to the married quarters which were located in and around the camp. I used to do my rounds, along with a wee Glaswegian pal from the Gorbals area of the city, on a little cart that had a small washing-machine engine attached to it. This coal-run was part of my fourteen-day punishment which I was still serving for some stupid mischief that I'd managed to get involved in within a day of arriving back at the barracks. After delivering the coal the pair of us were told to start up an old clapped-out cement mixer. Apparently we were to begin laying a surface on a stretch of road immediately. Within half an hour we were covered in cement and after the job was finished the grey cement and black coal dust made us resemble a couple of third-rate Al Jolsons. The punishment continued after the road-laying and we were flung into the cook-house to serve up the dinner. I was told to dish out the soup and wee McGuire was put in charge of the potatoes. The pair of us looked at one another, shrugged our shoulders and started the job. McGuire was too small to manhandle a massive pot of potatoes so he put the gigantic container on to the floor and began to mash them like hell. I could hardly see what I was doing because of the combination of cement and coal dust and, as I tried to rub my eyes and simultaneously acknowledge the corporal who had just arrived to check on our progress, my cement-laden cap fell off my head. It disappeared like a stone into the murky depths of the soup which was directly in front of me. I panicked when the corporal approached and I shoved the cap further down into the huge pot. The corporal sent me across the room for something but no sooner had I left when the cap floated to the surface right under the corporal's eyes.

"Right, McGinley!" he screamed. "You are dead, pal. Move it now!"

I was frog-marched off to the commanding officer's, pleading that I was *already* serving punishment. Just as I was leaving the kitchens my wee pal McGuire shouted, laughing to the corporal.

"Hang on a minute, you can take me as well!" Then he jumped into his big pot of potatoes and started mashing them with his steel toe-capped boots.

I got fourteen days' punishment and McGuire got fourteen days' jail for our culinary exploits. I subsequently heard that the cap was fished out of the soup and the identifiable pieces of cement separated from the grey lumps of potato before the meal was served as normal.

Christmas at Ripon was uneventful since most of us were assigned to guard duty. We listened to Little Richard's "Good Golly Miss Molly" on a radio owned by some rich guy who had gone home for the festive period and made some toast on an open fire in the billet. A wee concert party was laid on for us which starred some terrible English comedians who were unaware that their audience was made up of Scottish soldiers. We soon let them know who we were and they got booed off the stage after ten minutes.

We left Ripon on New Year's Eve 1957 and boarded a ship at Southampton later the same day. Over a thousand young soldiers stood on the decks of the T T *Dunera* as the vessel hauled itself away from the docks. I immediately took out my bayonet and started to carve my name and the date on one of the numerous highly-polished bannisters which everybody leaned on. Not for one moment did I consider this an act of vandalism. Napoleon's troops had chiselled their names into the Pyramids and like them I wanted to be remembered, I wanted to be part of history, I wanted the whole world to know that Ken McGinley went to Christmas Island on the last day of 1957.

Chapter Three

THE TT DUNERA wasn't the most luxurious of vessels and, as you might expect, any home comforts on board were conspicuous only by their absence. Our beds consisted of hammocks in the berths downstairs and wee Frank and myself made sure we were beside each other. Two other men called Harry and Chuck joined us.

A tall solidly-built soldier appeared through the wee door dragging his kit-bag and scratching his head. He promptly plonked himself down on another hammock nearby. We looked at one another in silence. Our huge companion slowly rubbed his face then said:

"Why don't us Scots all stick together?"

We weren't going to disagree with such a big guy so we just nodded in agreement. Then wee Frank walked over, stood on his tip-toes and squinted into the big fella's eyes:

"Okay, Tiny," he laughed, "join the clan!"

There was a moment's silence before the big guy laughed out loud. The name stuck to him and from that moment on he was known as Alan "Tiny" Robinson.

Chuck, meanwhile, was examining his watch. He said he'd bought it the last time he was back home in Paisley but some of us were convinced he'd nicked it as he certainly didn't have it when we'd left Ripon. He held the watch up to his ear to make sure it was ticking, then took a good look at the dial.

"It's Hogmanay," he drawled. "This is bad. We're stuck on a big boat out in the middle of nowhere. Jesus, this is really bad . . . ."

We shrugged our shoulders in agreement. Even if we'd had any drink to celebrate with, we couldn't have got near it since all our small bedside lockers were locked up. We'd also been ordered to have lights out at eleven o'clock sharp, so we reluctantly got into our pyjamas then climbed into bed. I think we were all feeling a wee bit sorry for ourselves at the time.

Forty-five minutes later, still dressed in our pyjamas, we jumped out of bed and headed for the toilets. We knew that we would never be discovered since all the officers were having a high old time of it in their quarters. I got out my harmonica and played "Scotland the Brave" at midnight while the rest of the boys belted out the words with glorious passion. Alcohol appeared from somewhere and we passed round a few bottles of whisky and some beer. The party was broken up by a couple of officers who had wandered downstairs but they were half-drunk themselves so they never reported us. As they walked out the door, wee Frank shouted after them:

"Happy New Year and I hope you both catch VD." (The cartoon-film we'd seen at Ripon, with the Hawaiian woman wearing a grass-skirt, had obviously not been wasted on Frank. Anyone who annoyed him was now liable to be told he hoped they caught VD. It was clearly the worst thing he could think of.)

A few days later the ship reached the Azores and by that time everyone on board had been sick at least once. Sometimes I couldn't make it to the railing in time and threw up all over the deck. I started to realise why decks were always being swabbed every time I saw a film at the pictures about the navy.

The galley was where the meals were served. There were over a thousand troops on board our ship so you can imagine the massive queues which soon built up at breakfast, lunch and dinner time. The crew were all Indian and they took a perverse delight in saying things which they knew would make young, queasy soldiers throw up. To be asked if you would like a runny fried-egg with greasy gravy poured over it first thing in the morning was not the most pleasant way to start the day. Later on we would always be given a plate of oxtail soup. The next day, once they'd sliced a few week-old onions into it, they would give us the same stuff back only this time it was called French-onion soup. That's what I call typical military improvisation. The five of us very rarely ate the soup but we always took it so we could spill some on to the floor. Then we would sit at the end of the long tables and have a laugh at all the other guys as they tried to keep their balance on the floor which had begun to resemble a murky skating rink as the ship lurched from side to side. Okay, it was cruel but at least it passed the time for us and I don't think anyone really got hurt – well there was that one poor English devil . . . .

The weather had begun to improve, the skies were cloudless day after day and the wind on deck lost that chilly edge which even the warmest of summer breezes always seem to have back home in Scotland. The five of us wanted to play football on the main deck and the sergeant said that he didn't mind just as long as we "didn't use a ball". Ha, ha, very funny . . . . When he heard this remark Tiny Robinson sloped off to our berths and returned with a home-made football manufactured out of rolled-up, smelly socks that he kept under lock and key in his bedside locker. This practice caught on and we spent the next few days playing our hearts out on deck. Obviously a few problems arose if the "ball" went out the "park" and we soon started to go through more socks than we had intended to. The game was eventually abandoned when the rest of the troops noticed their hosiery supplies were diminishing as those "bloody Jocks" played football day after day.

The weather became warm enough for us to sunbath on the decks and we used to throw water over each other to cool down if the temperature was really unbearable. I was lying with the rest of the boys one day when suddenly a message came over the public-address system requesting Mr Ken McGinley to report to the duty-room. The voice which made this announcement was unfamiliar and it didn't belong to the small-arsed disc-jockey who usually played the records. "Maybe somebody's kicked the bucket back home," said wee Frank as he screwed up his face and squinted his eyes against the sun. Somebody else grunted something about them finding out it was me who ran over the NAAFI cat at Ripon. "Thanks for the moral support boys," I thought as I headed for the duty-room.

Suddenly the orderly-sergeant appeared behind me with two other escorts and I was frog-marched into the captain's HQ.

"Are you, eh . . ." asked the captain, glancing down at a sheet of paper in front of him, " . . . Mr Ken McGinley?"

"Yes, sir," I replied quickly.

"Ah, so you're the gentlemen who carved his monica on my ship's hand-rail . . . ." he snapped.

The captain droned on and on about defacing the ship but I wasn't really paying any attention; I was just relieved that it wasn't any serious news from home. I was given extra guard duty and confined to ship as punishment. To be honest I couldn't have cared less. I was becoming used to landing in trouble and surviving.

Within the next few days we reached the Panama Canal. I can remember passing through the world-famous Milaflores Locks which lifted the ship up towards Panama City itself. As we neared them we were issued with our tropical kit which was to be worn when we left the ship at Panama City. As the TT *Dunera* went through the locks I

44

looked up at the banks and watched a group of little black children. All these cute kids had a transistor radio which played a rock-and-roll tune at full volume and as they listened to it they danced and giggled all over the place. We all laughed and waved at them and they returned out greetings with huge smiles and more energetic dancing. Apart from the films, they were the first black people that I'd ever seen in my life.

The TT *Dunera* arrived in Panama the following day and everyone received a pass for shore-leave and some extra money. Everyone except me that is. I was still in the dog-house for carving my name on the captain's much-loved hand-rail. But I managed to find one man who didn't want to go ashore so I asked him if he would loan me his pass for the duration of our stay in port. He immediately said he'd be delighted to help; the only problem for me was that this man was a half-cast. I decided to take the risk so I walked off the ship with as much confidence as I could muster and flashed the pass at the officer at the end of the gang-plank. He never even noticed the photograph on the pass and simply waved me off on my way. If he had queried the snap, I had prepared a story about having a particularly dark tan on the day the photograph was taken.

When we stepped on to the shore at Panama we were greeted by all the colourful locals, who came in every size, shape and bust-measurement that you can possible imagine. Each native had their pitch meticulously rehearsed for our arrival and they seemed to presume we were all very rich:

"You like to see my mamma or sister, man . . . only two dollars! Yeah, that's right, two dollars for you . . ." or "You wanna see a real special show . . . all nudes . . . no clothes, only one dollar! Just for you soldier, very special lady one dollar!" they purred.

We were more interested in finding the first pub to get a drink of decent beer or buying some postcards to send home, so we headed straight for the town centre on a little bus which had been sitting at the end of the pier. It took twenty minutes to reach the centre of Panama City . . . and what a city it was! It was like something out of a spaghetti Western. The culture shock was profound and we strolled around for hours with our youthful jaws hanging open. We found a pub with swinging doors like the type we'd all seen in cowboy saloons so we walked through them a few times for a laugh. It was far too hot to stay inside for very long so we bought a few bottles of beer then went on our way again. One of the guys decided to throw caution to the wind and sow a few wild oats so we had a whip round and gave him some US dollars and sent him on his way. Wee Frank was disgusted and reminded him about the film we'd seen at Ripon but the guy had had enough of living on a ship so he shrugged his shoulders and slunk off to see some wee Panamanian's sister or mother. Within a few hours we had no money left so we headed back to the ship. All four of us were beginning to regret not having bought any good souvenirs from the little man who had tailed us throughout our journey, waving his suitcase full of wares under our noses. By the time we reached the gang-plank we'd decided that enough was enough, so while two of us kept watch, the other two mugged the vendor and hopped off with a few handfuls of trinkets. Goodbye Panama.

The ship hit the sea again on 15 January for another couple of nights and our next port of call was Curaçao in the Dutch West Indies. The *Dunera* stopped here because our captain had accepted a challenge from locals to put up a cricket team from the ship against their First XI. We, as Scotsmen, couldn't have given a damn about cricket but we were grateful for the chance to stretch our legs again so we kept our mouths shut and acted like true cricket fans when the ship docked. As it turned out, the match was called off so we didn't have to endure the sight of our third-rate team being walloped by a bunch of wicket-hungry English exiles. Instead, we headed to a nearby beach where we found a lovely local lady had set up a wooden-shack which opened out into an idyllic-looking beach-bar. Wee Frank rubbed his hands together at the sight of the beer which was laid out on a bed of ice.

"This is free for all you soldiers," said the woman in faltering English.

"Well in that case," said Frank, "we'll take two."

The lady passed him two bottles of beer and smiled. Frank frowned at her and leaned over the wooden counter:

"I meant two *cases*!" he growled.

After finishing off the beer we hired a wee fishing boat from another native. The sun and the beer got the better of us while we fell asleep and drifted out to sea, basking in the midday heat. Frank soon took control of the situation and we began heading back into land. I woke up when the beach eventually came back into view.

"There's the shore!" roared a delighted Frank.

But I thought he said that we were *on* the shore, so I stood up like lightning and hopped off the side of the boat – straight into the sea in a drunken stupor. I couldn't even swim. Within minutes I was unceremoniously fished out and hauled back aboard the boat. That's what friends are for I suppose.

At the end of a long and eventful day we were gathered up by a couple of trucks which the captain had sent down for us. The journey back wasn't very pleasant. Everyone got sick at least once and some poor bugger shat himself. A brawl fired up as we boarded the ship and wee Frank ended up being slung into the *Dunera*'s jail. I was too drunk to visit him that night so I looked in on him the following morning when I'd sobered up a bit. He was lying in the cell trying not to throw up on the floor which was already awash with a sea of vomit. He was barely able to reply to my concerned questions so I left him alone in the darkness while I headed upstairs to the heat and the blinding brightness of the open deck. I wrote a letter home describing my life on the ship as it sailed towards Christmas Island:

> It is now four days since we left Panama City . . . I'm sitting on "C" Deck listening to the news. Last night we slept on the open decks as it was far too warm to sleep downstairs. We don't pass any land until we reach Christmas Island now. We have taken a good number of photos since we came aboard. I heard that we were on television the night we sailed from Southampton, one of my mates' girlfriends wrote and told him. We will write as soon as we have settled in on the Island. The weather at the moment is terrific, it's so warm that our dress is PT shorts with plimsolls. We went to see "Reluctant Heroes" last night, it was a good laugh.

Frank soon recovered from his stomach problems and the pair of us were assigned to night guard duty around the ship's decks. Sometimes we were able to get a few hours' sleep when no one was looking but more often than not we were kept awake by the Indian crew who used the deck for saying their prayers. We would be trying to doze off when suddenly half-a-dozen Indian cooks would appear. Then they'd kneel down on little carpets and start chanting. Two other soldiers who were on guard duty were also kept awake by this but they didn't have our patience; they stole the carpets and flung them overboard in an attempt to stop the chanting. Needless to say it proved to be unsuccessful and the Indian cooks returned the following night – "flying carpets" or no flying carpets.

After three weeks at sea we were collected together on the main deck and given a talk by a Sergeant Ward. He was a tall man with a large old-fashioned moustache and a passion for reciting bawdy stories, much to the delight of the soldiers under his command. I noticed on this day, however, that he was much more serious and subdued.

"Our main reason for going to Christmas Island," he stuttered, "is to [pause] witness bomb tests. Don't ask me what kind," he continued, "but I do know that they will be rather big."

After Ward's speech we dispersed and headed for our berths. We had only a vague idea about these "bomb tests" which the sergeant had mentioned. Our reason for going to Christmas Island was to participate in "Operation Grapple" which was so-called because:

> We have four main arms, civilian scientists and three military Services. For this reason we have chosen as our emblem the four-pointed grapple carried by a cormorant which is frequently used as the symbol for inter-service co-operation.

These words belonged to the Task Force Commander, W. E. Oulton, and they were contained in a small booklet entitled *Operation Grapple*. I knew I would be involved in handling machine-plants when I arrived at the island since that was the task I had been trained for at Ripon but I had no idea what these "bomb tests" were going to be like and, to tell you the truth, I wasn't really caring. I trusted my officers and was sure we would be well looked after throughout our stay on the island. I was secure, in my naïve belief, that my superiors knew what was going on, even if I didn't. Anyway, the little booklet on "Operation Grapple" had a foreword written by Aubrey Jones, Minister of Supply, which seemed to cover all the important points:

> In the absence of international agreement on methods of regulating and limiting nuclear test explosions – and Her Majesty's Government will not cease to pursue every opportunity of securing such agreement – the tests which are to take place shortly in the Pacific are, in the opinion of the Government,

essential to the defence of the country and the prevention of global war. They represent in their scope the minimum necessary to ensure that our weapons shall be powerful and effective, and a real deterrent to a potential aggressor.

Given the fact that "bombs" usually involved some sort of explosion, I was reassured to read the second paragraph:

No effort has been spared in the organization of the tests to ensure the safety of personnel involved, and to obviate danger to persons and property. The arrangements made to this end will be continued throughout the operation . . . .

* * *

It was four o'clock in the morning when I heard someone shout that land had been sighted. I dressed as quickly as I could and immediately made my way up on to the deck. A sight second to none greeted my bleary eyes which soon adjusted to the half-light of the dawn. In the distance I could see the outline of the island. Rows of lights, similar to those you might see on an airport runway, ran the length and breadth of the strip of land. Between us and the shoreline I could see the waves breaking in a foamy crescendo as they exploded against the coral-reef. The TT *Dunera* slipped through the water towards her anchoring point and, as the dawn sun slithered high into the sky, I began to see the outlines of palm trees swaying in the morning breeze. As the shoreline came closer and the sun shone like a white diamond in the sky, I looked in astonishment at the water below us. This wasn't the muddy, freezing and treacherous North Sea; the water was transparent and sparkling in the sunshine which allowed us to view all the marine life. Before long the ship was close enough for me and the rest of the excited soldiers who'd arrived on deck to pick out long rows of light-brown tents dotted along the coastline. Some small, matchstick-like figures, dressed in tropical combat gear, flitted in and around the shoreline. Some LCMs (landing craft) began to skip across the waves towards the ship where they would form our welcoming committee. I took one last look at this scene before going down to the berths and preparing for disembarking. Christmas Island looked like a bit of paradise which had fallen off and landed on earth. It was too good to be true.

The island had been discovered on Christmas Eve 1777, hence the name. When viewed from an aircraft it takes the shape of a gigantic lobster's claw. At its highest point it stands only ten feet above sea-level, it is only two degrees north of the Equator, 3,600 miles from California (the nearest mainland) and 4,000 miles from Australia. The temperature never falls below 75°F at night and frequently rises to 120°F during the day. All in all, it is a long way from Johnstone.

The LCMs came alongside the TT *Dunera* and we had to shin down a rope-ladder to board them. I was a non-swimmer and since my drunken escapades in the Dutch West Indies I was apprehensive of water. The landing craft bobbed wildly and there was a considerable gap between them and the side of the boat as I tried to jump to safety. Eventually I made it in one piece and I can't remember any accidents during the whole operation. We were soon on the beach and the officers sent us to our designated areas.

I was stationed at an area officially known as Port London, although we just called it Port Camp. It was run by the navy so it was also referred to as HMS Resolution. There were a couple of dozen soldiers from the RAF stationed there, as well as marines and a detachment from the Fijian army. The Fijians were the most friendly bunch that you could ever meet and they were really easy to get along with. They weren't allowed any alcohol from the NAAFI so we always bought them a couple of cases of beer and they, in turn, taught us how to catch crayfish and lobster. Sometimes they would come over to our tents and sing a few songs for us while one of them strummed a guitar. Later on, when I got to know some of them really well, they gave me an honourary Fijian title; they called me "*SonaLekaLeka*". Every time I walked by the camp, the large Fijian soldiers would shout this name at me and I would smile and salute them. (Nearly thirty years later I would be told that this meant "Little Scottish Short-arse"!)

The roads around this location were made from hard-drying mud from the numerous beautiful lagoons which were dotted around various parts of the island. Our camp had some buildings which had been constructed from prefabricated material brought from Britain. There was a fuel storage depot, refrigeration plant, cookhouses and other bits and pieces, including a beach-cinema, for our use. There was also a NAAFI canteen and bar, along with a small village where the native Gilbertese islanders lived. My tent was about two hundred yards from this little village and I had about five Gilbertese men working with me in Port Camp. They did mostly labouring for the services and they worked damn hard. I became very good friends with one of them who was called April McDonald. He told me his grandfather was Scottish, which was highly unlikely given the fact that April was as black as the night, and he was always trying to impersonate my Glaswegian accent.

Tiny Robinson was given the same tent as myself along with six other guys. Wee Frank, Chuck and the other boys were sent to Port Paris, which was about five miles along the mud-road. It didn't take long to settle into the camp and we were soon given our duties and told what we were expected to do during our year-long stay. I now had my very own bulldozer, a Fowler model, which I decided to name the *Ann-Marie* after my little niece back home. She was delighted to see a picture of me sitting astride the machine with her name painted in large capitals along one side. I was responsible for loading and unloading the landing crafts which brought the supplies into the island from the three merchant navy ships which were named *The Wave Ruler*, *The Wave Crest* and *The Wave Sovereign*. As I started my first morning's work I noticed that the TT *Dunera* was pulling away from the shore where she had been anchored for a few days. I watched all the people who were standing on her decks as they waved to us. The majority of those who waved with the greatest enthusiasm were soldiers who were on their way home. Every one of them had put in time on the island and they knew what we were in for. They all stood there, waving and shouting, as the ship sailed over the horizon. I was glad to see the back of it.

I had already started to write home to Alice, the young girl who I'd met before I left Scotland. In one letter dated the 5 February 1958 I described my new surroundings:

> Well Alice we have been on the island now for four days. It's quite good here. I hardly ever see Frank as I'm working in Port London and Frank is up at the other Main Camp. It's quite a big island and its very warm. Today is the best day of our week (pay-day!) and that also means a "bevvy" tonight. I went up to the main camp last night to play football and I met Frank there and all the boys too, but I had to leave early as I had no lights on my truck.
>
> I'm on constant night-shift now so I may go for a swim in the lagoon this afternoon then get a couple of coconuts for work tonight and I better not forget my bevvy either!
>
> The food here is murder and the tea has always got at least half a pound of sand in it. We can buy canned fruit and sweets. Cigarettes are 2/6d for Capstan, a big difference from British prices eh? I'll have to get a packet of Daz to wash my pyjamas tonight . . .

In another letter sent some ten days later I'm already beginning to feel quite at home:

> Thank you for your most welcome letter which I received yesterday. I'm sorry I didn't answer sooner as I was a bit dizzy last night (I was out for a bevvy . . .).
>
> I went to see Jack Palance in "The House of Numbers" last night. It was quite good. I'm sitting in the Fijian tent just now [The Fijian navy] one of the boys asked me who I was writing to, when I said it was to my girl, he sang "Only You" as I sat back and thought of you.
>
> I've just arranged for someone to take my films for development so I promise to send some as soon as I can. I've been told to get a hair-cut at least ten times this week. I've not had it cut since eight weeks past, the sergeant-major said he doesn't like "Teddy Boys" with their DA and Tony Curtis hairstyles.
>
> I've just came back from the cook house, there was nothing to pinch tonight and I'm starving.

Discipline on Christmas Island was very lax. If we did a late shift, for example, then it was very common to see men working on their equipment with a six-pack of beer beside them. Even if an officer or sergeant approached, they made no effort to hide the fact they were having a drink. The tents were sufficient for eight men with a small locker at the side of each bed for personal effects. The bed itself was a small canvas camp-bed which folded up and you also had a mosquito-net over it. Because of the heat we only needed a couple of sheets for bedding. We hung our clothes up wherever we could. The food was awful and we never saw anything that was remotely fresh. When anybody went on leave to Hawaii they used to bring back three or four pints of milk which would subsequently be raffled among the men. We were always given powdered eggs for breakfast which tasted of chalk. In fact, I believe most of our food actually dated back to the last war, so we were fed on Second World War rations. We actually survived on the food which could be purchased in the NAAFI canteen; at least we could spend our wages there on real food like chips and the odd sausage.

Because the quality of the food was so irregular we often suffered from stomach complaints like diarrhoea or constipation. To combat these illnesses a lot of us used to buy tins of Del Monte fruit-slices or fruit-cocktail from the NAAFI. After we'd eaten two or three tins of fruit we would finish the night off by downing the diluted beer which could also be purchased on the island. We weren't allowed to buy any spirits though – that was reserved for the higher ranks. So while the officers got drunk on a better class of liquid, the rest of us from the swinish multitude got stoned on third-rate shandy. This class difference was rather silly in my opinion since whatever way you look at it we were all trying to reach the same destination as quickly as possible . . . oblivion.

Entertainment facilities on the island were extremely basic. Most free nights were spent watching films which were shown in the Port Camp cinema. I've always been a great film fan and I really enjoyed all the pictures which were laid on for us. The "cinema" consisted of rows and rows of wooden planks which were arranged in front of a simple projector screen. Night after night we would all dutifully line up and watch whatever was on offer. Usually the selection wasn't too bad. I remember watching a young unknown actor called Paul Newman play a boxer in a film called *Somebody Up There Likes Me*. A couple of guys got carried away after that one and a few fist-fights broke out. Nobody meant any harm. It was just their way of killing time, which really dragged. I can also remember seeing a Marilyn Monroe flick during a really hot period in the height of the summer of 1958. Everyone was sweaty and uncomfortable, a condition not helped by the large land-crabs which crawled all over the place and the sight of the delicious Marilyn. (Don't forget there were over ten thousand men in one place at one time.) Halfway through the picture, the beautiful Ms Monroe appeared on screen wearing very little in the way of clothes. This brought all the usual wolf whistles and cat-calls from the young crowd. But just at that moment, it all got too much for one guy. The explosive cocktail of heat, beer and Marilyn's cleavage, pushed the guy to the edge of insanity. He bounded over every plank in the beach-cinema, stepping on countless heads on the way, before he finally took a flying-leap straight through the screen and into the outstretched arms of the Hollywood star. We were going to kill him. The pictures got cancelled for a week. The poor guy never lived it down and every one ribbed him about it for days. I think we were all secretly jealous.

I was always a great footballer and I regularly took part in the matches which were organised there. The pitch was a mixture of fine coral and sand which gave you a hell of a burn if you took a sliding tackle at another player. In fact, I still carry two bad scars from this sort of play during my stay on the island. I managed to play for my regiment, the army and even my "country" when we organised England v Scotland games to kill the time. Everyone took things seriously when these matches were held and the odd brawl after the fixture wasn't unheard of.

Every Sunday we would all troop off to hear Mass said in a little makeshift chapel. I actually looked forward to this since it broke the monotony and allowed everyone a few moments peace. There was never any problem about religion whilst I was on Christmas Island apart from the odd bit of harmless fun now and again. One of the boys from Govan, for example, heard me sing a few Irish Rebel songs during one of the hottest nights of July 1958. The next morning, while I nursed a hangover, a small crowd began to parade up and down the beach banging a drum like hell and trying to squeeze a tune out of a flute they'd stolen. The English troops didn't have a clue what was going on. I suddenly realised what tune they were playing . . . "The sash"! The half-wits had organised a wee "Orange Walk" on 12 July to get their own back at me. When it dawned on me what they were doing I laughed and laughed. What else could I do but applaud their ingenuity? The whole lot of us got legless in the NAAFI that night.

With hindsight I've always felt a bit sorry for the guys on the island who found it a wee bit difficult to mix. I was the complete opposite, of course, and I really enjoyed the company of my friends who played a big part in helping me complete my stay. Some men, however, really got it bad and it must have been awfully difficult for them to keep going. I spent most free nights, after the pictures or football, down in the NAAFI where I got drunk with the other guys. I was never a great drinker or smoker before I was posted there but I soon got going when I arrived. There was simply little else to do to pass the time. I suppose I thought of the trip as nothing more than one big, innocent adventure. My skin turned chocolate brown from the sun and my dark hair turned an unbelievable shade of blonde. I was at the peak of my physical fitness, a state I would never reach again. Some of the other guys, especially the married men, really got it tough during their stay. Some would receive a letter from the wife and family, perhaps containing a little snapshot, and they would just sit and stare at it for hours and hours. The rest of us always left them alone to their thoughts. Sometimes all hell would break loose when someone received a "Dear John" letter from the girlfriend who'd decided to call it a day. That happened a few times and it was more to be pitied than laughed at. We kept our mouths shut on such occasions knowing our own turn could come with the next post.

I grew up quite a bit during the first six months on the island. I was definitely at my best then. I had something pure and special inside me. I can't explain it in words. Whatever "it" was it soon went and I never found the time to appreciate and cherish it. I had to let go of the gift that money can't buy . . . youth. A person or persons unknown to me had decided that I was ready to watch the bombs. As far as the scientists were concerned the show was only starting but for me, and God knows how many others, it had already ended.

Anticipation and tension mounted steadily when we realised the first bomb test was imminent. The official date for the test was towards the end of April but preparations were well underway when I put pen to paper in a letter to Alice dated Monday, 23 February 1958:

> My dear Alice,
>   Just a wee note hoping to find you in good health and keeping out of mischief. Well Alice, the work is now pouring in for us, that's the reason I haven't written sooner. The boats with equipment for the bomb-test are rolling in. I've been towing low-loaded trailers of hydrogen all morning and part of the afternoon, I could have carried on but my bulldozer broke down. All the famous British Scientists and brain-boxes arrived last night in a Comet Plane. Sorry if I'm talking or writing something that might not interest you Alice but that's the only things I know that go on.

By the time I wrote back to Alice on Thursday, 17 April at 10.30 p.m., I was already beginning to worry about the implications of these tests. The officers didn't tell us much about them; they probably just didn't have any information and a noticeable aura of trepidation begins to invade my correspondence:

> I've got a lot on my mind at the moment Alice, there's a bomb going off thirty miles from here. It's the biggest any country in the world has ever attempted to set off. Believe me Alice, we're not out here for a pleasure cruise. The worst has yet to come, so between you, the bomb and us I don't know where we stand. There's boys writing out their last will and things like that, so you can't imagine what I've got in my big thick skull. I'm sorry if I'm kind of frightening you Alice, but I guess you are old enough to understand.

Before I recount the experience of my first nuclear bomb test which took place 28 April 1958, I would like you to read a brief article which appeared in the *Soldier* magazine. This piece was published in the March 1959 edition, some eleven months after my first bomb test in April 1958. Although the article does not specifically refer to the 28 April test it still infers that its author was present at one of the tests that year. I find this article highly intriguing for several reasons which I will mention later but for the moment let us examine the description of a bomb test in 1958 which the article's *un-named* author reputedly witnessed:

> A Sapper of 38 Corps Engineer Regiment describes how the troops live on the Army's farthest-flung and loneliest station: Christmas Island, a coral atoll in the middle of the Pacific Ocean where Britain is testing her nuclear weapons.
>
> The count-down begins and then, at last, the voice says: "The bomb has left the aircraft. Five, four, three, two, one, FLASH!"
>
> On the word "Flash" we feel the warmth on our backs as if someone had passed an electric fire behind us. The commentator counts on and then come the words we have been waiting for: "You may turn round now and face the burst."
>
> We turn and see a ball of fire, brighter than the sun. We shield our eyes. Gradually the brilliant ball fades to yellow, deepens to orange, rising rapidly in the sky all the time and leaving behind a white column that will soon become the stalk of a gigantic mushroom. The mushroom slowly takes shape, white and fluffy and unreal. We gaze in wonder.
>
> Suddenly we are jerked back to reality. "Stand by for the blast," warns the commentator and we get ready for the blow. But at that distance, all we hear is a big bang. We feel nothing more than a slight movement in the air and we continue to watch two Canberra aircraft fly right into the middle of the mushroom, sniffing for information which is vital to scientists.
>
> Some of us in the 38 Corps Engineer Regiment have spent many hours in the forward areas immediately after a megaton-bomb explosion, wearing protective clothing to keep out radio-active dust and carrying dosimeters to record the Rontgen rays. But contamination is negligible. My total dose to date is about the same as I get from my luminous wrist-watch every fortnight of my life.

If I didn't know better I would think that this was a very full and graphic description of a nuclear bomb test in the Pacific Ocean, written by a member of the armed forces who was actually present when the tests took place in the 1950s. But I do know better and from personal experience I can assure you that witnessing a H-bomb test was nothing like the events described in this magazine article. This is what happened to another twenty-year-old sapper from 38 Corps Engineer Regiment who was also stationed on Christmas Island in 1958; his name was Ken McGinley.

A glorious dawn broke over Christmas Island on 28 April 1958. I stuck my head out of our squat little tent on that morning along with hundreds of other servicemen who were taking part in Operation Grapple. Even at that early hour the tropical sun's rays were hot enough for us to move around shirtless and the sky was full of ugly cormorant sea-birds whose image decorated the operation's emblem. As I watched them flying around I never guessed for a moment that later the same day I would shovel up hundreds of their corpses with the eyes burned out of their pointed-heads after they too had witnessed a megaton nuclear explosion.

We were given a simple white cotton suit to pull on over our shorts and shirts while others just stood with their long trousers and khaki jackets. The sailors and the marines were, for the most part, dressed in normal gear with no special protection. This was to be the first nuclear bomb test which I'd ever witnessed and it would be the one and only time I'd ever be issued with any form of protective clothing. People claim we were issued with scientific equipment in the form of little badges or dosimeters which measured the levels of radiation we were exposed to but in my personal experience this did not take place. To this day I've still to wear one of these metering devices. I've also seen photographs of men wearing futuristic-looking goggles with hoods, taped-up seams and special boots who were reputedly stationed on Christmas Island during the nuclear bomb tests. Yet, in the year-long period I was on the island and throughout the five nuclear tests I witnessed, I never once clapped eyes on any such equipment nor, for that matter, any individual from the services wearing it.

On the morning of the test all the military personnel were gathered on to the main beach. We were told to sit down, relax and wait for further instructions from our commanding officers. The heat of the early morning sun made us very uncomfortable so we asked for permission to remove our cotton suits. But they told us to "Shut up and be quiet".

As I sat on the beach I started to become increasingly worried and all sorts of crazy thoughts raced through my mind. Two days previously I'd helped the Gilbertese villagers, most of the Fijians and the two WVS ladies, aboard the "safety-ship" HMS Messina. The Gilbertese couldn't wait to board the ship since they'd been promised the chance to go below decks during the test to watch Donald Duck and Mickey Mouse cartoons. As I helped one of the little WVS women to disembark from the landing craft she turned to me and said sweetly:

"We will pray for you all, God Bless."

These words had hit me like a slap on the face. I had never thought we were in any sort of danger until that very moment. But, as the date of the bomb test neared, lots of other soldiers who were braver than I ever was also started to get worried. I wrote home to Alice and outlined my fears in no uncertain terms:

> Before it [the H-bomb] went off hundreds of boys went down on their knees to pray, I joined them and prayed to spare everybody's lives and prayed that our love would never die. It was a frightful experience Alice, I hope I never go through it again. The reason for my starting and finishing my letters as a friend was because I was scared of what would happen when the bomb went off. I wanted you to think that we were friends, although I am very much in love with you. The reason being if anything would have happened I was hoping you wouldn't take it as hard if we were "just friends". But now I love you more than ever Alice, so never fear about getting friendly letters again.

This illustrates the psychological condition I was in as the tension mounted minutes before the test took place. Suddenly, before I could have any more misgivings, a voice came through the tannoy:

"This could be a live run," it said dramatically. "Five . . . Four . . . Three . . . Two . . . One . . . Zero . . ."

There was a moment's pause. Then it happened.

"Cover your eyes!" bawled the voice from the loudspeakers.

I had my fists shoved into my eyes and my back to the area where the bomb was going off. At the moment of detonation there was a flash. At that instant I was able to see straight through my hands. I could see the veins, I could see the blood, I could see all the skin tissue, I could see the bones and worst of all, I could see the flash itself. It was like looking into a white-hot diamond, a second sun.

Then the heat came. A slow, intense, searing heat which ate its way into your very bones. It didn't feel ". . . as if someone had passed an electric fire behind us". On the contrary, it felt as if someone had passed an electric fire *through* us. I let out a scream with the scorching pain.

"Okay, look at the bomb now," said the voice from the PA system.

The whole scene was unbelievable. A gigantic, dirty-looking mushroom cloud was forming on the horizon. An enormous ball of fire inhabited the base of the cloud and deadly-looking ripples of waves began to emanate from its base. It headed directly for us as we stood on the beach. I quickly glanced around me at the other men just as we got hit by a gale. Some tents got wrecked and the cookhouse collapsed.

"Did you see those trees snap in half?" I spluttered to one guy.

"A bloke over there has shat himself," said someone else. No one laughed when he said this. We were all frightened ourselves and our own bowels were in uproar. A man directly in front of me suddenly started to cry like a baby. A silent, low-level panic had descended upon even the bravest of men. I was worried about Frank. I didn't know if he was safe or not.

Immediately after the blast I glanced towards my sergeant who was standing there shaking his head in disbelief. I was perplexed with this reaction since I always assumed the higher ranks knew what to expect, but from this sergeant's expression it appeared he was just as shocked as I was.

I returned to the tent for a few things then headed towards my bulldozer when suddenly a torrential downpour began. By the time I reached the bulldozer it had eased off a bit but the controls were soaking and I had to wipe large dirty puddles off the seat. Although I was shaken, I managed to mount the bulldozer and carry on with my normal day's work. Concentrating the mind on simple tasks cuts through a lot of dangerous psychological confusion.

The details contained in the above description of the events leading up to and during the 28 April bomb test could probably be applied to any of the 1958 H-bomb tests I witnessed on Christmas Island. It is far more accurate, in my view, than the piece which appeared in the *Soldier* magazine. That particular article did not mention the apprehension amongst many of the soldiers before the blast, the lack of effective protection during the blast nor, indeed, the subsequent damage as a result of the post-detonation winds. The paragraph which compares the risk of radioactive contamination to the radiation contained in any ordinary luminous wrist-watch is so condescending it's almost below contempt.

The general public in the United Kingdom were kept informed about the progress of the Christmas Island bomb tests via some rather guarded articles which popped up from time to time in the British press. *The Times* ran a piece the day after the 28 April detonation which, like the *Soldier* review, had all the hallmarks of an official Whitehall press release. The article in question was presented thus:

ANOTHER BRITISH
NUCLEAR TEST
CENTRAL PACIFIC EXPLOSION
NEGLIGIBLE FALL-OUT

A British nuclear device was successfully exploded at a high altitude over the central Pacific yesterday. It was announced last night that Mr. Aubrey Jones, the Minister of Supply, had received a report from Air Vice-Marshal Grandy, task force commander, Christmas Island.

It was stated scientific measurements were being collected for accurate evaluation, and that early indications were that fall-out would be negligible. The device was dropped by a R.A.F. Valiant commanded by Squadron Leader R.N. Bates.

An Admiralty statement said: "Four warships and two Royal Auxiliary vessels make up the Royal Navy's contribution to the nuclear test programme in the Christmas Island area. In addition the Navy is manning Port London, where its base has been given the ship name H.M.S. Resolution.

With the assistance of Army personnel, naval officers and ratings have been responsible for the administration of the port and for the discharge of stores from ships bringing essential equipment to the three services.

H.M.S. Resolution which is commanded by E. Bruce R.N. was commissioned on Christmas Eve last."

Our Science Correspondent writes:–

If this had been a normal atomic bomb test there is no obvious reason why it should not have been held in the Montebello islands off the Australian coast. There has been a widespread impression that an important British thermo-nuclear test was pending.

The article in the *Soldier* magazine and the above piece in *The Times* both fail to mention the possibility of local radioactive fall-out. They simply dismiss it as "negligible". I believe that this was incorrect. The heavy rain which I witnessed after the 28 April blast cannot be ignored. Admittedly there was nothing unusual about this phenomenon so I didn't really think much of it at the time. With hindsight, however, I am inclined to wonder whether this original assessment might have been a little premature. Predictably, the article in *The Times* never mentions this rainstorm nor the possible dangers which could befall anyone caught out in the open during it. (The piece in the *Soldier* magazine only mentions a "slight movement in the air . . ." which bears out my belief that the unidentified author has taken complete leave of his senses.)

Other men who were on the island with me also remember the rain. Several of them have openly expressed their doubts about the MOD's claims that it was harmless. Ken Taylor from London, for example, was a cook on Christmas Island during my stay there. He was based at exactly the same location that I was, HMS Resolution, when the 28 April bomb went off. He clearly recalls the events of that morning:

"It bucketed rain after that one," he says. "It was heavy rain . . . like liquid hailstones or even Singapore during the rainy season."

Another witness to the same detonation was a friend of Ken's from Birmingham, Tom Birch, who was also living under canvas at HMS Resolution. What he saw on the morning of the detonation will stay with him for the rest of his life.

> They delayed the test by about an hour because there was a cloud bank building up off the south-east point of the island where the test was due to take place. The cloud did not seem to have gone when the detonation actually occurred. Ten to fifteen minutes after the blast, as Ken Taylor and I walked back to the Port Camp, we suddenly became aware of a very thick black cloud approaching inland from the sea. It was as black as pitch. The cloud came over part of the island then retreated back out to sea again. By that time we had all been showered in rain which was as big as "ten-pence pieces". We all ran like mad to get away from the rain it was so torrential. Lots of men must have been caught out in the open though. Immediately after the detonation there was panic amongst the boffins. From the way that they were acting it was clear that something had gone far wrong. The whole thing appeared abnormal, unusual. Landing crafts and other vessels were being started up all around us so that we could be evacuated. As it turned out we never actually left the island, the rain sort of cleared up and we were left looking at each other. It all ended in complete chaos and confusion . . . I remember the sky the following morning, it was completely orange, almost like a martian sky.

Normally it was a brilliant blue colour. It was weird . . . totally unnatural.

But when one compares the above testimonies to a *Top Secret Ministry of Defence* report on 28 April blast, the contrast between our evidence and the official military line becomes even starker. This report, which has never been seen publicly before, was unearthed by the journalist Eamonn O'Neill when he was doing some research for this book in the Public Records Office.

The document refers to the 28 April megaton blast. It was written by Group Captain W. E. Townsend and it lists lots of senior officers and various important observers who were present during the preparations for the test and indeed the detonation itself; it also describes the bomb blast itself. Here are a few excerpts:

> The Task Force Commander ordered the next one as a live drop and the count down proceeded until the round was released at 1005 hours and burst at 8000 feet above ground zero, 57 seconds later . . . it was learned that this was a "clean bomb". *The air burst precluded any water or dust being drawn up from the surface which may give possible radioactive fall-out and it was not anticipated that any fall-out from this bomb would occur.* From the general security point of view it was not stated just what the megaton range of this round was, but it was quite apparent from the discussions and observations that it was the largest bomb yet exploded by the UK. [Author's italics]

As you can immediately see this document completely fails to mention the pitch black and that it rained after the blast on some parts of the island. It assumes, therefore, that none of the servicemen were ever in any danger of being exposed to radiation. I have always believed that this assumption could be challenged. Surely the fact that it rained after the tests proves that something went wrong? Why do none of the official accounts of this blast mention this rain? These are important questions which should have been answered. But they weren't. The MOD have always stated that the rain, if any existed, would not have done us any harm. They claim, quite fairly, that it often rained on the island. Why should we be so concerned about that particular rainstorm? The answer to this question and the reason why I question the MOD's stance is simple enough. Firstly, I believe all the men, including my own judgment, when they say that they instinctively knew that something was wrong. Secondly, I'm absolutely certain that the rain was radioactive and

I'm sure you'll agree when you read the following letter from Captain W. G. Stewart who, as a twenty-year-old RAF recruit, participated in the same 28 April test. His account of the blast reads as follows:

> I was co-pilot of a Shackelton, (Reg. 859), on a shipping patrol, 60 miles from the blast of an H bomb on 28th April 1958. The explosion set off a line of thunderstorms, below which we were forced to fly to return to Christmas Island. *There was torrential rain, which entered the unpressurised aircraft like a sieve, turning the only detector, a small rudimentary device on the captain's lapel, immediately to the wrong colour.* I believe that another Shackelton was caught in the same predicament.
>
> Both Aircraft were scrubbed for days, if not weeks, before a fast transit, or at least fast for a Shackelton, across the U.S.A. back to Ballykelly, Northern Ireland. On that trip, starting 15th May 1958, I flew 856, which could have been the other involved. Weeks, perhaps months, later some bright medic realised that if the aircraft were irradiated then, chances were, that they had contained crews at the time, therefore we were given a blood test, apparently a pointless exercise unless a pre-exposure comparison has been done. [Author's italics]

Saying that the rain on that day might have been irradiated is one thing but actually proving how it could have come about is quite another. Only a scientist could do that. This important issue was addressed in part during an interview which Professor Joseph Rotblat, Emeritus Professor of Physics, University of London, gave when he was interviewed on the BBC's *Nationwide* programme when it dealt with nuclear test veterans in the early 1980s.

Professor Rotblat attended pioneering experiments during the Los Alamos tests in the United States and is widely regarded as an international expert on radioactive fall-out. In the course of his television interview he was asked about the safety of air-burst detonations of a nuclear weapon. An "air-burst" detonation involves a warhead which is detonated high above the earth's surface. Most scientists agree this is safer than a "surface-burst" which is detonated on the ground, like the Nevada tests in the United States. A surface-burst generally lifts up enormous amounts of surface-matter and therefore leads to widespread radioactive fall-out when it's dispersed back to earth after the mushroom cloud has formed. The Christmas Island tests, however, did not involve surface-bursts – instead air-bursts were used to simulate an air-attack on a military port of strategic importance.

Authorities have always believed than an air-burst does not suck-up a large amount of surface-matter and consequently the subsequent radioactive fall-out is negligible. These common assumptions were challenged by Professor Rotblat during the course of the interview and his answers underline my belief about the nature of the puddles I cleaned after the 28 April bomb test:

> . . . generally it's assumed that there is no local fall-out at all if the explosions take place at a high altitude but this is not quite true because there are possibilities of some local fall-out occurring even with high altitude bursts.

Professor Rotblat proceeded to explain two examples of local fall-out which could occur after an air-burst. First, there is the "after-wind" effect, when a column of water is sucked up from the sea. This reaches the fireball where it mixes with radioactive materials and, under suitable atmospheric conditions, returns to earth in a radioactive state. Secondly, there is the "rain-out" effect. This occurs after the nuclear device has been detonated; when the fireball ascends it encounters a rain-cloud, mixes with the cloud's contents then returns to earth in the form of rain. Professor Rotblat concluded by stressing that these two examples could have more significant implications if the "air-burst" occurred at a *lower level than the scientists had planned*. As Professor Rotblat commented:

> If the explosion occurred at a lower altitude then of course the effects would have been much bigger.

But that was only half the equation. The real question which still existed concerned the precise height of the explosions that I witnessed. I thought that many of them were much lower than the experts had predicted. If this was correct then it would mean Professor Rotblat's theory about the possibility of local fall-out could possibly be applied. But how could I prove that these blasts were lower?

In 1988 a coroner's inquest would be held into a man's death. The deceased gentleman was named Collin Frederick Kendal Smith. He was an ex-serviceman who had spent almost exactly the same amount of time on Christmas Island as I did. We must have seen the same five tests go off during 1958. Like me, his first bomb test was on 28 April of that year. He died of cancer on 21 November 1985. During the inquest, the Coroner, Mr E. J. Wain, spoke to Dr J. Fielding from the Royal British Legion. In the course of this exchange the question of the height of the detonations was raised:

> *Fielding*: A great deal depends upon the height of the burst.
>
> *Coroner*: Yes, now these were high air-bursts, as I understand them.
>
> *Fielding*: Well when I saw the Ministry of Defence document on this subject they described four out of the five cases as high air bursts and I assumed that these meant high altitude bursts which is commonly agreed by experts in this area to be over a hundred thousand feet and in such conditions the amount of fall-out is accepted to be negligible.
>
> *Coroner*: Right now that is by distance alone isn't it?
>
> *Fielding*: The question of distance applies only to the initial radiation – we're talking about fall-out from all the debris of the bomb.
>
> *Coroner*: Yes.
>
> *Fielding*: Which can depend upon the conditions, I mean if it were a ground burst for instance then a lot of that would be almost immediate, within minutes, in the local area. At higher levels, it's dispersed over a much wider area and comes to earth perhaps in months or years. But as I understand from the latest bit of information which I've had put in front of us today, these air bursts were not so tremendously high as I had anticipated before and in fact the balloon, if I may refresh my memory, I see the balloon detonated bomb was at something like *1,200 feet*. Now this is not a great height. It is trust that one would not expect an enormous amount of fall-out from that but I can't convince myself in my own mind that at that level there would have been no fall-out whatsoever . . . [Author's italics]

Professor Rotblat's comments and the above extract from the inquest serve only to confirm what I believe really happened during and after the 28 April H-bomb test. But perhaps the most damning piece of evidence comes again from Glenn Stewart, the pilot who, as a young man, witnessed the 28 April blast. Eamonn O'Neill interviewed Glenn and asked him to detail his experiences about the detonation he'd witnessed.

> *O'Neill*: Can we now turn to the question of the height of the April 28 bomb?
>
> *Stewart*: Yes, certainly.
>
> *O'Neill*: At what height would you say that particular device was detonated at?

Stewart: It went off at 800 feet. Yes it was definitely 800 feet.

O'Neill: Are you certain it might not have been higher . . . several thousand feet for example?

Stewart: No. It was definitely under one thousand feet.

O'Neill: An official government report on that blast puts the height at 8,000 feet, what is your reaction to that?

Stewart: No . . . that's wrong. It was much, much lower than that. Definitely under one thousand feet.

If Glenn Stewart is correct than the above interview can only lead one to conclude that the official 1958 document, which lists the height of the detonation at 8,000 feet remember, has got its sums wrong. If this seems slightly fantastic, then one should take note of the following information which has only recently been uncovered by Eamonn O'Neill.

In the official 1958 Top Secret report on the 28 April test we are informed that:

> The ground zero for the burst was a point *five miles* off the south-east point of Christmas Island.

This language makes no room for any doubt. The facts that are presented go straight to the point, don't they? The bomb was detonated "five miles", or 8.047 km, off the south-east peninsula of the island . . . that's what we're told, so that's the way it must have been. Until the MOD changed its mind that is! At an inquest recently some documents were given out which listed the bomb trials, distances and heights, etc. One of the documents contained information about the 28 April test which included some figures about the distances off the island where the trials took place. This listed the ground zero area as being 2.5 km, or 1.5525 miles, off the edge of the island! Even at the most conservative estimate this revealed that the MOD was willing to reduce its original estimates outlined in the 1958 document by well over a half. Moreover, Glenn Stewart, completely unaware that the MOD had revised its figures, pointed this flaw out during his interview with Eamonn O'Neill. After he'd shown Glenn the figures about the height of the air-burst, Eamonn allowed Glenn to browse through a copy of the 1958 report. Without any prompting, Glenn spotted the error in the MOD's estimation concerning the distance of ground-zero from the island. Indeed, he suggests that the real point of detonation could have been as close as 1/4 mile or 0.40225 km away from the island.

This last piece of new evidence cannot be ignored. If the MOD are prepared to revise heavily its figures concerning the distance of the 28 April bomb when it was detonated, then one can only speculate about the actual height of the device on that morning. If, as I and many others believe, it was much lower than the 1958 document reports, then Professor Rotblat's rain-out theory can be applied. All the witnesses were interviewed separately and none of them were aware of the others' evidence. All of them spoke about the rain long before TV programmes mentioned the significance of it in relation to the rain-out theory. (Tom Birch's medical records, for example, clearly illustrate his belief that the rain had harmed him. This assertion dates back to 1983 which is a full year prior to anyone mentioning rain-out in public.)

As we shall see in later sections of this book, this information becomes even more startling when it is placed into a different context and its significance in the long-term is, to say the least, powerful. For the moment though let's return to Christmas Island in the days which followed the 28 April test.

Three days after the 28 April bomb test, I awoke to find my face, neck, hands and the upper-area of my chest covered in large water blisters. I made my way over to the medical officer's tent and queued outside with a line of other men who had similar complaints. By the time the medical officer examined me, my eyes were nipping profusely and tears streamed down my cheeks. He prescribed me with a bottle which sprayed a plastic-type covering on to the rash and a pair of sunglasses for my eyes. The rash cleared up about two or three weeks later but it left a noticeable scar along my chest and face.

One morning shortly after this I attempted to get out of bed only to find my right leg was refusing to move. Initially it felt as if I might have a bad case of "pins and needles" but then it went completely numb. I panicked and dressed as quickly as I could before making my way over to the medical officer's tent again. On the way over I became really frightened and I started to cry. The doctor said the best thing to do was to put the leg in plaster for a few days. His plaster fell off after two days and I found it difficult to move around on the island with two crutches. I was eventually taken into the medical tent for observation for a couple of days, with my right leg suspended in a sling. The patient in the bed opposite me was a sailor by the name of Tanky, who was suffering from coral poisoning. His shinbone had a hole in it where the coral reef had penetrated it. The wound was deep enough for me to have put two fingers in it. As we sat talking, one his pals came in to visit him. The moment I saw the guy I realised he had some sort of a mental problem but I didn't want to say anything to Tanky.

"It's a bit chilly in here," remarked Tanky's wide-eyed visitor.

After he'd said this he disappeared outside for a few moments before returning with a large piece of crunched up newspaper which he suddenly set light to. He casually proceeded to set the medical tent on fire. Thankfully someone appeared and all the patients were hauled to safety. This incident gave me a hell of a fright and the shock actually helped my leg, for within a few days it was much better. The guy who set fire to the tent was placed under medical supervision and escorted off the island.

After the bomb tests, discipline deteriorated rapidly and men would do anything to get off the island. I sat at breakfast with Corporal Ginger Redman one morning. He was looking rather ill and had been complaining of stomach pains, headaches and vomiting, so I advised him to report sick. Later in the afternoon I went to visit him but the doctor, an officer, wasn't going to let me in since he was sure Ginger was really skiving off his duties. I knew Ginger well and I realised dodging work wasn't his style so I persisted until he gave way and let me in. When I went in I saw poor Ginger lying on a bed with his eyes sunk in his head and his skin a jaundiced yellow colour. I whispered a few words into his ear but he didn't answer so I left with the intention of calling back a few hours later.

In the evening, after I'd visited Frank and NAAFI for a few beers, I walked the short distance to the medical bay. I looked at Ginger's bed but it was empty so I called over an orderly and asked him about it.

"He died an hour ago," he said flatly.

"Eh?" I stammered.

"His body's over there pal," said the orderly pointing to a bed in the corner of the tent.

I went over to the bed and pulled the single white sheet back. Ginger lay dead.

Some men who had arrived with me on the TT *Dunera* and who'd been stationed with me at the main camp were being sent home on medical grounds. Other men at my camp started to lose their tempers for the smallest reason whilst others just walked around in a trance all the time.

On my way back from the main camp one evening I noticed two servicemen standing in an area of scrubland looking up towards the sky. I stopped the truck and asked if they wanted a lift back to the Port Camp.

"No, it's all right, mate," said one of them calmly, in a soft, southern-English accent, "don't mind us, we're just talking to our new friends."

I looked around to see if there was anybody else but the three of us were clearly alone. After some strong words they reluctantly accepted a lift from me. As we moved off they started to cry because they said they were leaving their friends, the telegraph poles, behind. By the time we reached the medical bay I was starting to get a bit frightened myself but I held my composure long enough to drop the two soldiers off. I never saw them again and I heard later they were taken straight off the island for psychiatric treatment.

A week after this incident I was told I was entitled to a week's holiday in Honolulu. A crowd of us piled aboard an aircraft and left Christmas Island for the first time in six months. The island looked tiny when we saw it from the air, which was in total contrast to the view from the *Dunera* on our arrival. We didn't need to look through windows for our view since the pilot had left the aircraft's main door open. I was flying for an hour before I realised it was my first journey aboard an airplane.

Fourteen hundred miles later we arrived in Honolulu to be greeted by girls wearing grass-skirts and singing traditional songs. I was grinning like hell when one of them came over to me and placed a garland of flowers, called a *lei*, over my head. We journeyed from the airport to the US army barracks named Fort De Russey where we would stay for the duration of our holiday. I'd already made friends with a little guy from Liverpool called Spud Murphy so I wasn't short of company. The pair of us gasped when we saw our rooms in Fort De Russey. They were sheer luxury! The beds were lovely and soft, there were curtains on the windows and we had access to the base's dining facilities – all for only one dollar per day.

When we went out for lunch we visited Hickham Air Base which is near the infamous Pearl Harbour. Its dining-room had palm trees growing inside the eating area and all the officers and ordinary soldiers mixed together when they were eating, a total contrast to the class system which existed in the British Army. After we'd introduced our ID cards we were directed to the food counters. Our jaws hung open when we turned the corner. There were steaks an inch thick, pork chops and something called french fries. But best of all was the unbelievable selection of milk! I hadn't tasted real milk for months so I headed for it like a bullet out of a gun. There was strawberry milk, mint milk, banana milk, chocolate milk and good old white milk. I grabbed four pints for starters and settled down to stuff myself.

I spent two days in Fort De Russey near Waikiki beach. Spud and I went to a revolving bar one night and got legless on two drinks. To this day I still don't know how the bar actually revolved because I'd never been to a place like that before or since. The bars I frequented in Scotland only had revolving customers.

The following morning Spud and I went out on to the shore at Waikiki beach to play football. We kicked the ball around for a while then started heading it to one another. Some local children gathered around us as we played this strange game – they'd never seen soccer before of course. The next thing we knew, a photographer from the local newspaper turned up to take some pictures of us. A week later they were printed, along with an article about us, in the popular *Sunday Post* newspaper in Scotland. My mother was full of maternal pride when she read of our exploits:

YANKEE BIG-TIMERS
LEARN A
NEW SEASIDE PASTIME
And a Johnstone Lad Taught Them!

Ever heard of the fabulous Waikiki beach at Honolulu? The sun-soaked holiday paradise for American film stars and millionaires where nothing is too expensive if it means entertainment and pleasure for the wealthy visitors.

Well those dollar-happy holiday makers have just been taught to have a bundle of fun with nothing more expensive by way of equipment than a tanner ba' and no training apart from a lesson or two, in the guid auld Scottish game of "headies". And it was a Johnstone lad who did the teaching.

Kenneth McGinley is serving three years as a Sapper on Christmas Island in the Pacific and he recently went on a leave trip with a buddy to this wonderful Waikiki beach. A quick look around the golden sands, a dip in the warm azure sea and then, like all guid Scots, Sapper McGinley said, "Let's get the ba'".

This lad who lives at Lillybank House and was formerly employed with Wilson Bros., was an outstanding Secondary Juvenile with the St. Fergus Club in Paisley before signing on with the R.E.'s and he never loses the opportunity of a game – even in a place like Waikiki.

The upshot of all this was that he and his pal began a nice quiet game of "headies" on the beach, but before long they were

surrounded by a large crowd of enthralled spectators who watched
for a while until they finally demanded to be initiated into the
mysteries and technicalities of the game.

With the result that scores of millionaire bonces are now busily
engaged each day nodding the wee ball back and forth across the
sands of Waikiki.

Sounds like a cue for a song that – and who knows – we may
get one. Meantime, a Johnstone lad has taught the big time
Americans how to really enjoy a day "doon the water!"

Spud and I were a bit short of cash after our revolving bar escapades
so we went for a walk around the town to kill time. Two young,
clean-cut men approached us and asked if we wanted to make a bit
of easy money. We agreed and followed them to a local clinic where
we sold a pint of blood each for ten dollars. After I'd given the blood I
looked around at the rest of the customers in the clinic. They were all
deadbeats and poor-looking drop-outs who would have looked more at
home a decade later during the hippy era. I felt sorry for them and a
little ashamed of myself for actually selling my own blood but I needed
the money so I hung my head and left as quickly as I could.

On my third day I walked around the beach-front area and
approached a stall where a plump lady stood selling various items.
I pointed to something and asked its price:

"That's a dollar, honey," she replied.

I pointed to something else on the stall.

"And that's a dollar too, honey," she laughed.

I pointed sheepishly to another trinket in front of her.

"And I suppose that costs a dollar as well," I joked.

"It sure does, honey," she said, "'cos, this is a 'dollar-stall'."

The woman started talking to me and asked me where I was from
and how I came to be in Honolulu. When I mentioned Christmas
Island she perked up and appeared to know all about the bomb tests.
The next thing I knew, she had invited me back to her house to
meet her husband. I agreed and went to Fort De Russey to grab my
luggage.

When I returned she'd shut the stall and was standing next to the
longest car that I'd every seen in my life. It was like a large boat
on wheels and it had gigantic tail-fins like a spaceship. She drove
us to the drive-in restaurant called the "Kau Kau Korner" where her
husband and son worked. Both of them shook my hand warmly and
the son casually asked me if I would like a record specially played on
the radio. I said that that would be fine and I asked for one of Elvis

Presley's hits of the time. The next thing I knew the radio station was announcing my name and playing an Elvis record for me. I thought I was dreaming.

I stayed with this family, whose name was McGarry, for nearly the rest of my time in Honolulu. They had two lovely children called Joey and Timmy, both of whom I took an immediate liking to during the days that I looked after them. The McGarrys used to take me out on runs in their speed-boat which was called *Thumbs-Two*. I thought this was a strange name for a boat so I asked them why they called it this.

"My husband lost two fingers in his old job," laughed Mrs McGarry, "but they paid him compensation which is what we used to buy the boat. We thought we'd call it *Thumbs-Two* in honour of the missing fingers, without which we'd all still be on dry land."

The McGarrys' house was a magnificent glass-fronted affair with lots of windows and more breath-taking views than you could ever possibly imagine. They were always throwing parties and for the time I stayed with them I seemed to be the main attraction. Night after night a steady stream of visitors would file in to look at me and listen to my strange accent. I didn't mind this attention in the slightest; indeed, for a twenty-year-old from Scotland it was like walking on to a Hollywood film set.

I spent two days in Fort De Russey again before I left Honolulu. Mrs McGarry and some of the family turned up to see me off at the airport. They kissed me goodbye and gave me some small gifts as I boarded the aircraft. I was sad to be leaving Honolulu but I was still shrewd enough to buy plenty of fresh milk before I left which I was supposed to give to wee Frank when I arrived back on Christmas Island. I deviously changed my mind and raffled the milk instead. I made a clear profit of seven pounds with a clear conscience; Frank would have done exactly the same thing.

As soon as I returned to Christmas Island I heard a rumour about a sergeant who had died after witnessing a bomb test. The nature of this death and subsequent burial was a big talking-point among all the troops who had known him. After he'd died his body was placed into a makeshift coffin which had been knocked together by some soldiers on the island. The coffin was put on to a LCM and taken out to HMS *Narvick* so the sergeant could be buried at sea.

After a short journey out to sea the coffin containing the sergeant's body was tipped over the side of the ship into the clear-blue Pacific

Ocean. It soon became apparent, however, that the coffin wouldn't sink so some soldiers were ordered to shoot some holes into the side of the coffin. Much to the captain's horror the coffin still refused to submerge so it was hauled back on board. The troops had to bore some more holes into it and the casket was riddled with a few rounds of bullets before it was hurled into the sea again. Only then did it finally sink.

Stories like this inadvertently led to an atmosphere of sheer depression which spread rapidly throughout the camps. In the high summer of 1958 men began to drink more and serious grudge-fights broke out on a more frequent basis in the NAAFI. I found myself smoking more heavily than I'd every done previously. It was around this time when the orders were pinned to the board informing us that another bomb test was due to go off on 22 August. The test was given a press build-up by *The Times* in London:

BRITAIN TO MAKE
MORE NUCLEAR TESTS
STARTING DATE
NOT DISCLOSED

Britain is to resume her nuclear tests at Christmas Island shortly it was announced by the Ministry of Defence last night. No further details of the coming tests were given and the Ministry did not disclose when they would start.

Christmas Island – an isolated coral atoll in the Pacific – was chosen for Britain's first hydrogen bomb tests. The first such test took place high in the air over the central Pacific in May last year when the "device" was dropped from a Valiant four-engined jet bomber. The testing of further nuclear devices followed.

In April this year the successful explosion of a British hydrogen bomb was reported. Mr McMillan told the House of Commons that the test was in the megaton range.

Restrictions on traffic in the test area was lifted on May 3.

Earlier this month is was announced that Air Vice-Marshal T.A.B. Parselle had been appointed new commander for the task force "Grapple" which is conducting the Christmas Island tests.

When the day of the bomb test arrived we expected to be issued with the white cotton suits and to be lined up on the beach before the bomb went off. But as I sat on my bulldozer waiting for these instructions, I was told to forget about the bomb and carry on working as it was "only" an atom bomb. (This meant it was roughly similar to the bombs dropped on Hiroshima and Nagasaki.) No preparations were undertaken, no cotton suits were issued, no line-ups took place, nothing. Everything carried on as normal and I worked away on my bulldozer, stripped to the waist, wearing a floppy-hat and shorts as the time of detonation neared. Because the highest point in the island was only ten-foot above sea-level, I could easily stand on top of the Ann-Marie and take in an excellent view of the A-bomb test-site which was at the other end of the island. The bomb went off on time and I gazed at the initial flash then at the gigantic mushroom cloud that formed against the pale blue sky. I didn't think much of the explosion since it wasn't nearly as big as the earlier H-bomb which I'd witnessed in April. The wind which followed the August test didn't cause much damage and there wasn't any rain either. After it was all over I went back to work as normal.

The soldiers were never well informed about the bomb tests. We only found out about a test a day or two before it was due to go off. After the 22 August test we would witness another three nuclear experiments within the space of one month. Two of these would involve the detonation of the enormous hydrogen bombs. God only knows what psychological effects these tests had on the soldiers. I was really nervous when I heard I was going to witness another H-bomb test and I said so in my next letter to Alice:

> The bomb went off this morning, the one we have all been waiting for. It was the biggest and most successful megaton explosion ever set off in the world. It was a bit frightening and half of my tent-mates sat up all night when they heard it was the big one. I was scared Alice, no kidding. I guess it was that extra prayer that gave me a little more courage.

The 2 September test was carried out using a similar procedure to the other H-bomb detonation in April. All the soldiers were taken down to the beach at dawn, ordered to sit down and then told to wait for the blast. The crucial difference, however, was that none of us were given any white cotton suits. In other words, we witnessed a massive H-megaton explosion wearing shirts and shorts.

We knew what to expect with this second bomb test so we weren't as shaken up as we had been with the previous one. The damage in and around the camp was just as bad, though, and after the test took place we returned to find our tents in a real mess as a result of the wind which immediately followed the blast. The NAAFI had its windows blown in and the cookhouse collapsed again.

Another H-bomb was detonated nine days later. By that time I was ready to go home. I know for a fact that some men committed homosexual acts in the hope they'd be caught, charged and sent back before another bomb test. Other men also acted completely out of character. My big pal Tiny Robinson, for example, became broody and the pair of us almost came to blows one night after we'd had a bad argument. During the argument we suddenly realised what we were doing so we stopped dead in our tracks. Nobody said a thing, they didn't have to. Everyone knew that the pressure was mounting. Tiny, like the rest of us, just wanted to go home to his family. Nobody criticised his brief loss of temper; family men were respected on Christmas Island and everyone knew how hard it was for them.

About a dozen or so Fijian soldiers were kept on the island during the bomb tests in September 1958. We were friendly with one of them called Albert. He was a massive big guy who could work us all under the table any day of the week. A few hours after one of the September bomb tests Albert was found sitting on a deserted beach trying to eat the coral which had been washed up on to the shore. Albert knew this could have killed him but he still kept shovelling it into his mouth. Two of us grabbed him and tried to stop him harming himself but as we got him to his feet he started to cry loudly:

"SonaLekeLeka," he sobbed to me, "I wannna go home, I don't want to stay in this place, please take me home, away from this place, please!"

Albert was placed in solitary confinement for a few days before he was finally removed from Christmas Island.

The military personnel on the island often ate various types of fish which could be caught in and around the shore. I was taught to catch cray-fish by some of the Fijian soldiers and the Gilbertese villagers. This practice continued before, during and after all the nuclear bomb tests. After the September tests, for example, we often visited the spa, an area of the sea near the shore-line which was next-door to the testing area. We fished this area for cray-fish the day after the last two or three bomb tests. And as many witnesses will testify, the bird and marine life suffered heavy casualties after the tests. At Port Camp, for example, I was assigned on a couple of occasions to collect the dead birds which were lying all over the place. I personally collected about fifty which had badly singed and scorched wings. Others were half-dead but were blinded by the explosion so they just flapped their bruised wings as they lay in a pathetic heap on the mud roads. On closer examination, you could see that their little eyes had been burned out of their sockets. It was really horrible. I collected some marine-life which was also washed up on the beach along Port Camp. Some sharks had managed to find their way through the waters around the treacherous coral-reef, more by luck than design probably, and were beached on the shore. They were dead by the time I reached them but you could clearly make out the distinct scorch-marks which ran along one side of the poor creatures. The burning flesh gave off an awful stench. I later spoke to some crew members of the *Wave Crest*, anchored near the coast, and they told me that following the initial blast they'd seen hundreds of dead fish floating around the coral tempting all the hungry sharks from the open sea where they normally fed.

The last nuclear bomb I witnessed was on 22 September 1958. There were no special preparations for this test and I watched its detonation from the seat of my bulldozer, the *Ann-Marie*. Apart from my normal working togs (ie, shirt, shorts and boots) I had no protective clothing.

By the autumn of 1958 I was falling ill more frequently than I'd ever done in the past and I was in a state of confusion about my career in the army. After the 2 September bomb test I awoke to find my voice had completely gone, my throat was on fire and I had a severe cough. My neck was also badly swollen. I was told to drink lots of cold water but that didn't really help. By 15 September it was established that I was allergic to penicillin and that my glands were severely swollen. It took the medical staff on Christmas Island over a month and a half before they realised I was really ill. On 28 October I was admitted to Tripler US Army Hospital on Honolulu suffering from chronic tonsillitis. During the intervening months on Christmas Island I had felt very uncomfortable yet was still forced to do hard quarry work. On 29 October I underwent an operation to remove my tonsils. I was as nervous as hell before going into theatre because I always had my brother Jimmy's death at the back of my mind. He had died on the operating table while having his tonsils out so I didn't write to my mother in case she got upset. During the operation I woke up and looked at the surgeon just as he was placing my detached tonsils into a small jar. He smiled at me and told me to go back to sleep again; needless to say I refused.

A few days after, I noticed there was a problem in the muscles in the right side of my face. I became really worried about this and called the doctor over to examine me. He diagnosed a condition called "Bell's Palsy". I returned to Christmas Island where I was fitted with a splint in order that the right side of my face might be elevated to a comfortable angle. My condition improved over the next few weeks and I managed to get rid of the splint within a fortnight or so.

Everybody was desperate to get off the island as soon as possible. Some of our kit was sent on ahead of us but we still kept a spare outfit for our journey back to Britain. Some other troops had already arrived on the island to relieve us and they quizzed us about conditions on it. We didn't want to rub too much salt into their wounds so we said that it hadn't been too bad during our eleven-month stay. This optimism wasn't all a front for we heard there weren't going to be any more bomb tests so we knew the next bunch of soldiers wouldn't go through the same fear and apprehension which we'd all had to endure.

Some troops left Christmas Island via ships like the *Captain Cook* or the TT *Dunera*; others, like us, left by air. On 15 December 1958, after spending 351 days on the island, I boarded an aircraft with Frank, Tiny and other troops. During this time I'd witnessed five nuclear bomb tests. As our plane took off I settled back into my seat and closed my eyes. I refused to take one last look at Christmas Island as the small aircraft circled it before heading towards Honolulu. To be perfectly frank about it, I was just glad to see the back of the fucking place.

* * *

Our return journey was broken up into several legs. We stopped in Honolulu first in order to refuel the plane. This gave me the opportunity to call up the McGarrys and a local girl who I'd met when I was on leave there. The McGarrys never made it down before I left but the girl showed up with a gigantic garland of flowers for me. I dutifully wore it as I said my goodbyes to her but the moment I boarded the aircraft all the guys started shouting names and singing love songs to me. I was sad to leave Honolulu that afternoon. It was a really beautiful place which appears to have been somewhat exploited and spoiled by the hordes of tourists who have since visited it.

Our next stop was San Francisco on the West Coast of America. It was the very first time I'd ever been in the United States and it was an experience I'll never forget. The contrast between Christmas Island and San Francisco was like black and white. The city was at its post-war height when we saw it; all the buildings were made of spotless white brick, the pavements were gleaming, massive cars which guzzled the endlessly cheap petrol cruised by, the gardens in Union Square were full of sightseers and people walked around at night without fear of being disturbed. We were able to view the complex freeway interchanges against the skyline of the city with the famous Golden Gate Bridge forming a frame to the whole scene. It was magnificent.

As Frank and I walked into our hotel we noticed a tall, bald-headed man standing in the foyer. Frank walked up to him and prodded him in the chest:

"You're that big, baldy guy out of *Dagwood and Bumpstead* aren't you," he laughed, but before the poor man could reply Frank spat out a catch-line from the American TV programme: "Don't go Near the Water!" he shouted at the top of his voice.

"Where the hell do you come from?" asked the tall man.

"We're from Scotland," replied wee Frank, "and you're in that programme aren't you? You can't kid me, pal . . . you're the boss, the big, baldy boss . . . 'Don't Go Near the Water.' Ha, ha, I watch that *Dagwood and Bumpstead* all the time!"

"Yes," said the man, "that's right, my name's Fred Clark."

Both of us got Fred's autograph before we went to our room on the twenty-fourth floor. Wee Frank was delighted.

The excitement of going home meant neither of us were able to sleep that night so we ended up ordering breakfast at three a.m. After I'd stuffed myself with pancakes and maple syrup I went for a quick bath while Frank lay on the bed. I was in the bath for no more than two minutes when suddenly there was one hell of a rumble. The building shook like hell. I thought Frank had maybe fallen out of bed or done something he shouldn't have.

"What's going on?" I screamed from the bathroom as I pulled on my robe.

"I don't know! But whatever the hell it is I don't like it . . . get out of here now!"

The pair of us got dressed and ran to the nearest lift. It took ages for the elevator to reach the ground floor and by the time we finally got there the whole foyer was teaming with people running to and fro. Within another half-an-hour the front pages of the early morning newspaper headlines ran "EARTHQUAKE HITS CITY!"

Two days later we left San Francisco and flew to Dalouth, Minnesota. The journey was awful for wee Frank since he was suffering from toothache. Our sergeant kept telling him to eat something and the nice stewardess waved scrambled eggs under his nose every two minutes but he would have none of it and spent the entire flight under a blanket growling unintelligible oaths at anyone who dared annoy him.

The arrival in Minnisota was a hell of a shock to all our systems. Indeed, when I think about it now it's hardly surprising that so many of us got drunk during the trip home. We'd left an island that Robinson Crusoe would have found lonely, thousands of miles from anywhere, and within twenty-four hours we'd been dumped in the middle of San Francisco, one of the largest cities in the world and prone to earthquakes every so often, and then flown into a small town called Dalouth which had temperatures of twenty below! It had taken us nearly a year to become used to tropical conditions and now we were instructed to run across the runway tarmac in case we froze up. Everyone was confused that night and to make matters worse we'd been warned not to talk to anyone about our experiences on Christmas Island and never divulge descriptions of the bomb tests we'd witnessed.

We stayed in Minnisota for two nights then we flew on to Newfoundland in Canada. The weather was even worse there and the snow drifts reached at least three feet high. Some local girls invited us out when we arrived and it was here I tasted my first ever milk-shake.

A couple of days later we flew from Newfoundland back to London. When we arrived back on British soil I think we expected to be treated like some kind of long-lost heroes. I knew there had been lots of publicity about the bomb trials in the British newspapers and that all the scientists were proclaiming the wonders of this so-called "Atomic-Age". We saw ourselves as pioneers at the forefront of this new age – we'd actually seen a bomb go off so we knew from first-hand experience what the new military deterrents looked like. If the politicians were right and this device would allow us all to live in safety for ever and ever then surely we deserved some credit for being around when they tested the damn thing. But when we arrived back at London Airport the first thing we encountered was a line-up of grouchy customs men who didn't give a damn where we'd been or what we'd seen exploding. Our uniforms didn't seem to be worth much. We were all really desperate to get home, yet here we were being held up by a wee man looking for some fags that Frank and I had planked inside our luggage. I even had to pay duty on a radio I'd bought to keep me company on Christmas Island. Nobody gave a damn about us.

We went straight to Euston Station and hung around waiting on the next train to Scotland. We finally caught a train to Glasgow which took a longer route than normal. The ticket inspector said that we should have taken an earlier, more direct, train. We protested and said that it didn't matter since we all had army travel warrants but he insisted and charged us all an extra two pounds. By that time everyone had had enough so we paid up in silence and settled down to catch some sleep before we reached Glasgow.

Just in case you think we're exaggerating our feelings concerning our return journey I would like to point out that years and years later I found a newspaper article from *The Times* dated 1958 which highlighted the case of some other soldiers in a strikingly similar situation to ours. After I had read the article I grew even more angry since it illustrated the cold-hearted and calculated fashion in which all us returning soldiers were treated. The article ran as follows:

"LIKE PAUPERS"
SERVICEMEN HAD TO
BORROW IN U.S.

Three British service men arrived last night from Christmas Island, Britain's nuclear weapon test base in the Pacific after what one of them described as "a terrible journey".

The men were Sapper P. Cleeland Royal Engineers and a sergeant and a corporal of the R.A.F. Sapper Cleeland who had a fractured knee in plaster and was using crutches as a result of an accident said there was no one to meet them in New York, and no accommodation had been arranged. They had to borrow $10 each from the British Consulate to pay their hotel bill. "We got to New York at 9pm and didn't get into bed until two in the morning," he said.

The R.A.F. sergeant said: "We felt like paupers. For a whole day on the journey from Honolulu to New York we had only a few sandwiches. We hadn't any money. We were told before we left Christmas Island that signals had been sent ahead and everything would be looked after."

In New York they had to pay $6 each for a bed and "that left us just about enough for a couple of cups of tea".

After visiting the sick bay, Sapper Cleeland left in an ambulance. The R.A.F. men who have completed a tour of duty on Christmas Island travelled to London.

A spokesman told *The Times* last night that no complaint had yet reached the War Office and therefore there could be no official comment. There had been few, if any complaints from men returning from Christmas Island and it would seem that there was some special reason for any discomfort experienced by these men on this occasion. Perhaps the authorities were more concerned with getting the men home than getting them home in comfort.

An Air Ministry spokesman said that men leaving Christmas Island were given a subsistence allowance, but it was not clear whether these three men drew the allowance which was "something of the order of £15".

After an awful train journey we finally arrived in Glasgow to find the place much the same as we'd left it almost a year before. But each of us had changed inside and in our own way we knew it. For months and months we'd planned and fantasised about what we'd do when all we wanted to do was go home and go to sleep.

I caught a bus to Johnstone along with a few other lads and I waved to big Tiny as he got off at Paisley Cross. As he saluted me with his massive hands I never imagined for one moment that I wouldn't see this gentle giant for almost thirty years. I continued my journey with only a snoozy Frank for company until we finally reached Johnstone a few stops later. It was a rainy and cold 22 December 1958 and I was glad to be home.

Two nights later I went to midnight Mass. Going to a Christmas service in my home church, St Margaret's, was something I'd often dreamt about when I'd been on Christmas Island. The thought of proudly wearing my uniform as I walked through the church door with an air of confidence and having a calm, settled mind had been a private vision which had frequently pulled me through many nights of loneliness and terror during the bomb tests.

Halfway through the Mass, as I sat five rows from the front, I began to see flashes of light and hear loud sounds in my ears. I turned to say something to the person sitting next to me but I was already falling to the floor. I passed out in front of the whole church and had to be carried out of my seat. When I came to, I was shivering and shaking like a leaf; it was the first time in my life that I'd ever fainted.

After New Year I returned to Ripon. Although I was looking forward to seeing all the boys again I knew my heart wasn't in it any more. I constantly felt ill and it wasn't any surprise to find myself being admitted to Caterrick Military Hospital with a bad flu-type illness at the end of February 1959. I stayed there for approximately four days before I was discharged back to Ripon. My next posting was to Otterburn in Northumberland where we had to build a road deep in the damp countryside. It was a very lonely place and we stayed under canvas for the whole period. I didn't feel very fit either and the fact that we only got terrible rations made me feel even worse.

One night, while I was staying in the tent in Otterburn, I woke up with a start and went into a series of painful spasms. The front of my pyjamas felt damp so I sat up in bed and examined them. I was drenched in a pool of blood. Someone put me on to the back of a motorbike and rushed me to a local hospital where I was given an injection to make me sleep. I remember them telling me I'd suffered internal haemorrhaging. When I woke up the next morning a dirty old doctor shoved two paracetamol tablets into my hand and gruffly told me I'd be all right. I was discharged ten minutes later.

I returned home to Scotland that same weekend and visited my own doctor in Johnstone. He said I was in no fit state to return to active service but I did attempt to journey back down to Ripon after my weekend leave was finished. My girlfriend Alice accompanied me to Central Station in Glasgow on the Sunday night but I felt too unwell to tackle the rest of the journey so I about-turned and headed back home. I was in a hell of a state.

My local doctor supported me with a series of long-term sick-notes and I was admitted to Cowglen Military Hospital, which is just outside Glasgow, in the summer of 1959. I was put through a whole series of rigorous tests which eventually led the doctor to diagnose a serious duodenal ulcer. I spent sixteen days recovering there before I was discharged and sent back to Ripon to be examined by an army doctor. I was told I was being discharged from military service on the grounds of "Ceasing to Fulfil Army Medical Requirements, Para 503 (xvi) (b) (11) Q.R. 1955."

I still attended a local doctor on a regular basis who took a special interest in my health. He was particularly concerned about my ulcer and the fact I shook and sweated continuously for no apparent reason. The first time I visited him as a civilian after being discharged from the army, he examined me and shook his head.

"What's wrong, Doctor?" I asked him.

"You're such a young man," he said sagely, "and you'll always regret the day you ever set foot on Christmas Island . . . ."

Chapter Four

I WAS HOME from the army for only two or three months when I heard that a friend of mine by the name of Tony Crampsey had fallen ill after returning from Christmas Island. I had known Tony for a number of years and I'd actually bumped into him on the island a few weeks before I myself had left. He was always a healthy guy so I was shocked to learn how ill he really was when I visited him.

"What's wrong with you?" I asked him.

"The doctor can't really find out what the problem is," he answered. "I've had skin rashes around my neck and when I was on the island I had to wear my light uniform constantly to cover myself up. I've never been right since I came home."

After I'd chatted with Tony, his sister Elizabeth pulled me to one side.

"The doctor says his glands are in a terrible state," she whispered. "That's where the root of all his problems are and the prognosis isn't good either," she added.

I said my goodbyes to Tony and left him alone in the front-room of his house with only his pain for company. He would suffer, on and off, for the next two decades, defying medical opinions about how long he had to live. He was one of the bravest men I've ever met.

Immediately after I arrived home I began my search for security and peace of mind. Back on civvy street I was uncertain where my future lay. I suppose my chaotic health had a lot to do with it and I wasn't able to do a lot of the things that I'd always taken for granted. I found playing a full game of football, for example, a real effort, yet only a year before I had been sought after by teams in the army and at one point I had a chance of playing with a semi-pro squad in England.

In December 1959 I made one of my better decisions when I asked my girlfriend Alice to marry me. I think I proposed to her when we were standing in a close somewhere – anyway, she said "yes" and we were married in St Margaret's Church, Johnstone, on 23 April

1960. Alice decided to take religious instruction in order to start the process of converting to Catholicism so the problem of mixed marriage disappeared. I did compromise a bit though . . . the wedding reception was held in the local Orange Hall!

My employment situation was extremely precarious so we ended up living in my mother's large house in Brewery Street, Johnstone. My brothers, Danny and Davie, had also moved in with their wives. I loved this arrangement and remember the time I stayed in "Lillybank" with great affection. Apart from feeling constantly ill, I was confused and a bit frightened at that time so living with my family gave me security and helped me to get back on my feet.

My first job after I got married was in a paper-mill factory in Johnstone. I worked in the stock-room as a general labourer – well that was what I was supposed to do. The moment I reported for my first day's work I knew there was something wrong with me. I found it almost impossible to settle down and I resented any kind of authority from my managers. I couldn't stand being confined to one place, the lack of space frightened and annoyed me, and I was desperate to get outside to open spaces. I lasted a couple of months in this job. I took another couple of local labouring jobs within the next year or so but I still couldn't calm down. In many ways it was a vicious circle; the more I tried to settle the more difficult I found it. I made matters worse by thinking there was something wrong with the jobs when in fact the real problem lay with me.

I eventually found myself taking a job with the local carrying firm, Wilson Brothers. I had worked there after I'd left school and before I'd joined the army, so I was delighted to start with them again and to be working alongside wee Frank Murney again. I thought that everything would work out fine now that I was back to my old job again but I couldn't have been more wrong. I fell ill with nausea, dizzy turns and my hands kept swelling up at the oddest times. I was constantly taking powders and pills which didn't seem to be doing much good and the doctors still couldn't pin down what was really wrong with me. I walked out of that job one day and took another as a salesman with a sausage company. I worked for a few months there before taking another job with a crisp business, which I stuck out for a short time before eventually beginning work as a bus-driver for Western SMT Ltd. I enjoyed this job and stayed with it for three years until I finished in 1965. Then I moved to a job as a driver with a catering supply company which had the added incentive of providing me with my own transport in the form of a wee van. I loved this job, mainly because I was able to be by myself and take the little company van home at night and at weekends. I found it increasingly difficult to work at close quarters with other people though and my patience ran out quicker than it ever did in the past. My temper wasn't helped by the fact that I still fell ill all the time. I was in constant pain, with horrible large boils that suddenly appeared all over my body. They were purple in colour and I had to go to the doctor a few times to have them lanced. The stuff that came out of them was disgusting. Neither I nor the doctor knew what they were but I remember noticing that they were near my old water-blister scars which had appeared after the bomb tests. An extract from my medical records illustrates the problems I was having:

> At present off work . . . In June 1961 was referred to Casualty Department, R.A.I. Paisley from his work on account of severe abdominal pain but was discharged home the same day. No other hospital treatment. Obtains powders from Doctor for stomach pain . . . Pain is accompanied by nausea – no actual sickness. Pain is frequent at night causing sleeplessness.
>
> About August 1962 was admitted to Western Infirmary and had operation to stomach [part of stomach removed] . . . off sick for three months. Previous to this admission had been frequently off work on account of disability. Complaint: Troubled with "wind" after eating, can only eat small meals, appetite is easily upset. Gets easily tired and feels weak.

My wife Alice was really wonderful with me throughout this bad patch. Not only did she take care of me when I fell ill but she also put up with my moods when I moved from job to job. She even helped me with some nightmares which I suffered from, especially a recurring dream about my military service. In the dream I was only nineteen years old and I was working on Christmas Island. I would walk back to my tent and open the canvas door to find my friend, Peter, standing looking at me. I would stare in horror at this apparition before saying to it:

"It can't be you, Peter, you died in the lorry crash in Germany . . . It can't be you, you never came to the island with us, please go away, please."

Then I'd wake up suddenly in the bed with the sweat running out of me and with Alice telling me to calm down. It was terrible and this is the first time I've ever told anyone about it. It's a period in my life that I'd rather forget.

From 1967 onwards I was, thankfully, much more settled. Alice and I decided to try and have a family but we soon realised there was something wrong. I immediately assumed that the problem must lie with Alice since all my brothers had by this time fathered large families. Alice went for a check-up with the doctor and came home with the unexpected news she was absolutely fine and there was no reason why she shouldn't be able to have children. I immediately went to the doctor and then to the hospital for a series of tests which confirmed that I had an unusually low sperm count. I was absolutely devastated and racked my brains for possible reasons as to why this had happened. At the time I could find no answers. Only years later did I discover that exposure to radiation can cause impotency. My year on Christmas Island meant that Alice and I would never produce our own child.

I worked with the catering equipment firm until 1969, when they offered me a position of assistant branch-manager in a new outlet they were planning to open near Durham, in England. At the time Alice and I were living in a small flat in Johnstone and I was desperate to move on to better things. When I was really ill I used to promise Alice that, given the chance, I would "get myself together" and work hard. All I'd ever really wanted out of life was a semi-detached house, a car in the garage and a family. It wasn't much to ask for and, with the offer of a new job, I thought that it might be within reach.

In December 1969 we headed off to England. It was a terrible night when we tearfully left Johnstone, and we barely made it through the winds which were whipping up around the Beattock Summit near the Border. By the time we'd actually reached Durham the following morning, our clapped-out old Ford Cortina, with all our belongings packed on top of it, was ready for the scrap heap.

Initially my job wasn't too bad but both of us were finding it difficult to settle down. I found my drinking had become a bit heavier and I still had difficulty sleeping at nights. By 1973 I felt that my mental state had deteriorated rapidly. I was threadbare, worn out and on the edge of a breakdown. I'm convinced that these problems developed because I was ignoring my physical problems which had started to become much worse again. My joints ached constantly, I felt sick in the mornings, I suffered insomnia, my teeth had fallen out, I shook for no apparent reason and I broke out in heavy sweats. Things came to a head when I suddenly collapsed one day when I was driving a company car. I ended up in hospital with severe kidney complaints which the doctors could find no apparent reason for. I recovered enough to be discharged within a couple of days and I returned home to Alice a day or two before Christmas 1973. When I walked through the door I realised that the pressure of my constant ill-health was beginning to get too much for Alice as well. She threw her arms around me and started to cry so I asked her what was the matter.

"This will be the first time I've ever been away from home at Christmas," she sobbed.

I hesitated for a minute or two then I decided to pack our bags and go back home to Johnstone. When I told Alice about my decision she smiled and laughed:

"I've already packed . . . "

Almost as an after thought and just as I was about to start the car, I went back into the house and called my boss:

"Hello, who's speaking?" he said when he answered the phone.

"It's McGinley," I shouted, "and you can stick your job up your arse!"

I slammed the receiver down and grabbed the car keys on my way out the front-door, not even bothering to look back. I'm not proud of my actions but that was the state of mind I was in at that particular time.

Alice and I returned to Scotland and we stayed with my mother for about six months. My personality underwent a bit of a change at this time and I found myself going for long, long drives in the car at night. It wasn't that I wanted to get away from loved ones or anything but I suppose it was just my way of trying to get some peace of mind.

I frequently drove down to Dunoon on the West Coast of Scotland to look at the places where I used to spend my holidays when I was a child. The route to the little town takes you through some of the most remarkable scenery that you could ever possibly imagine. There's one point on the road which is just beyond the "Rest and Be Thankful" mountain-pass that I really love. On every side you are surrounded and enveloped by the magnificent Highlands. A little stream, filled with perfectly clear water, runs by the side of the road under an ancient-looking stone bridge. I'd sometimes stop the car at this point just to take in all this natural beauty. The space and the awesomeness used to wash over me and I always felt better when I fired up the car's ignition and continued my journey down the road to the coast.

One particular day after making this journey I decided to go for a walk around Dunoon's main thoroughfare. The town had changed a bit from the days when I used to visit it as a child. Lots of similar little seaside towns up and down the coast of Scotland had literally died during the 1950s and '60s, simply because the "never had it so good" generation had all upped and gone abroad following the advent of the affordable package tour. But Dunoon was totally different. I found the town bursting at the seams with young American couples who were stationed at the nearby US navy base. All the little shops on the main street were crammed full of consumer items which suppliers would never normally have sent to the owners. Within a hundred yards I passed four or five public houses and half-a-dozen prosperous-looking restaurants. There were at least two or three packed laundries and I couldn't believe the amount of American accents that I heard during my walk down that one street. All these people had travelled in from the specially-built US personnel houses which were located on the outskirts of the town, arranged in neat-looking schemes. As I walked further down I could hardly believe the number of taxis which I found lined up waiting for customers. When I mentioned this to a newsagent, he laughed and said that Dunoon had the highest amount of taxis per person in the whole of the British Isles. I smirked at this silly idea until he said that he wasn't kidding. On the sea-front itself there were rows and rows of lovely guest-houses which appeared to be doing plenty of business with the Americans who needed temporary accommodation until they found permanent digs. I was really delighted to see the old place thriving and I just kept walking and smiling. For the first time in years my mind was clear and I really felt that things were starting to look up.

As I made my way back to where my car was parked I happened to see a small house which was up for sale, so I went in and had a quick look around it. The house was called "Glensloy" and it was the bottom flat of a detached house. I felt that it might have some potential as a guest-house. On the journey back to Johnstone I made up my mind actually to buy the place using the money I'd made on the deal after selling the house in Durham.

Alice and I moved in a short time later and immediately started cleaning the house out. We started a small bed-and-breakfast business and became good friends with some of the lovely local people who lived nearby. Business was brisk with plenty of casually dressed Americans passing through our books on a regular and profitable basis. In fact, the flat above ours was leased out for a period to an American couple with a large and very noisy family who succeeded in driving Alice and I round the bend.

We stayed in "Glensloy" for about three years before we decided to move to a larger property which was right down on the shore-front.

Alice and I loved the place, "Pitcairlie", from the first moment that we saw it and we realised its prime position would be excellent for business. Prior to moving I had been working in a local TV shop as manager but I decided to pack that in and work full-time in the bed-and-breakfast business instead. Alice and I loved the guest-house and we worked hard in "Pitcairlie" to build up a good clientele.

Although I really enjoyed my work in Dunoon I still missed not having a young family to share it with. To make up for this gap in my life I occasionally used to invite some children from a local Catholic children's home called "Nazareth House" to stay with us for the weekend. It all began as I was driving past the front door of the home one night when I was feeling especially lonely. I stopped the car, went straight in and spoke to one of the nuns who looked after the children. I asked her if I could possibly take one or two of the children home with me for the weekend. Unbelievably, she agreed to let me take two little girls back to Alice for a couple of nights. I used to do this on a whim and I soon became well known to the nuns in Nazareth House but deep down I knew it was no substitute for having your own family.

By the late 1970s Alice and I had already made a few enquiries about fostering and adoption. We went as far as making a formal application to the St Margaret's Adoption Society in Glasgow but unfortunately this was turned down. I refused to stop hoping and we decided to make a last-ditch attempt at adoption through the local social services. After we'd gone through the interview procedure we heard nothing for some time so we went abroad for a holiday for a couple of weeks. When we arrived back we were informed that we were to call a number that had been left for us. After that we were told to travel immediately to the offices since they had some good news for us. Within three days we had a beautiful seven-month-old daughter named Louise.

A few months later I received a letter concerning my war pension. Since my discharge in 1959 I had been in receipt of a moderate pension because my ulcer had been classed as being "attributable" to service. The letter which I received in 1980 stated flatly that my pension was about to be cut. I was upset about this since my ill-health could be traced back to my military service on Christmas Island. Moreover, the fact that I'd never been able to undertake a physical job meant my earnings had been dramatically curtailed in the years since I'd left the army. My unstable behaviour throughout the period hadn't helped matters either so I decided to appeal against the decision to axe my money. To cut a long story short I was unsuccessful and my pension was reduced to twenty per cent.

My two-yearly pension assessment rolled around again in 1982 and I decided to appeal against the earlier decision to cut my money by ten per cent. Two things had happened during the intervening years which had made me reach this decision. First, a lady from Dunoon had given me an extract from a magazine about a man in Canada. The individual in question had suffered a whole range of different illnesses since he'd arrived in Canada after emigrating from the United Kingdom. Whilst I read through the article I suddenly realised that the pattern and nature of these medical complaints were startlingly similar to the problems I'd been encountering over the years. In fact, I'd go as far as saying it was like looking in a medical mirror. The main difference between us, however, was that whilst I had been unable to father children this man had a family of two, both of whom had been deformed. The most interesting feature in this man's biography, as far as I was concerned, was that he'd been in the army and, most important of all, he'd served on Christmas Island during the nuclear bomb trials. The magazine which carried this article was called *Sanity*, published by the Campaign for Nuclear Disarmament (CND), an organisation which I'd only vaguely even heard of. But after reading that magazine article I began to ask myself some serious questions, questions which I knew I had no real answers to.

The second reason why I decided to appeal against the tribunal's decision involved my medical records. I was entitled to see my records in order to give myself a fair chance to prepare a case to argue at the hearing. The records I was duly supplied with were supposed to be a detailed record of all the treatment that I'd ever received during and after my military career with the Royal Engineers. As I leafed through the sheets of paper I realised that there were a few discrepancies covering the period when I'd served on Christmas Island. The records appeared to say nothing about my "frozen leg" which had developed after the bomb tests and which had caused me so much distress. And the records appeared to say nothing about the severe "body rash" which had emerged after the bomb trials and had caused me a lot of pain and subsequent scarring. I felt that these omissions should be explained and that no decision about my war pension should be made unless they were recognised and taken into consideration.

I went along to my hearing in June of 1982 and made a statement in front of the three-man tribunal which held its meetings in Glasgow. I told them about the omissions and said that this led me to believe my medical records were, more or less, incomplete. I said that I did not know why such important and relevant details had been left out but I nevertheless felt all my medical and psychological problems dated back to my service on Christmas Island during the nuclear bomb tests. I was absolutely certain that I'd been exposed to harmful radiation during all these tests, I said. On that basis, I concluded, I should have my pension increased by ten per cent to its original level of thirty per cent.

When I'd finished my statement the three men thanked me for my time and said that I would be informed about their decision in due course. Within a few days I received a letter which bleakly stated that my pension was staying at the decreased level of twenty per cent. When I realised I would still only receive approximately fourteen pounds per week I was shattered. I was physically and emotionally drained and I knew the authorities expected me to give up my struggle and simply fade away. But something inside me told me I was correct in my belief that there were more cases similar to mine and that, up and down the country, there were other men who had been ill since they'd returned from Christmas Island. It was at that moment that I made one of the most important decisions I've ever made in my life. I chose to stand and fight my corner no matter what the consequences were.

One night in November 1982 as I sat alone in the house in Dunoon I reflected on some conversations that I'd had with some old army friends from Johnstone. One guy I'd known all my life had told me a disturbing tale of the depression he'd suffered after returning from Christmas Island. Only a week after arriving home he'd walked into a local dance hall and, for no apparent reason, started a riot. He was promptly arrested and flung straight into the local police station before he was brought up in front of the judge the following morning. When the judge asked him to give an explanation for his irrational conduct he immediately answered:

"It was the bomb tests on Christmas Island that made me do it, Your Honour."

I knew this man and I realised he wasn't kidding when he'd said this. As far as I was concerned it was an all-too-familiar scenario and I couldn't help thinking, "There but for the grace of God go I."

Other men I chatted with had broadly similar tales to tell so I decided to get out a small writing pad and send a letter to the *Daily Record* in Glasgow. I addressed it to the "reader's page" which ran about six or seven letters every day. The letter asked if any readers had suffered medical problems after they'd returned from the bomb tests on Christmas Island. (I naïvely assumed that the Christmas Island tests were the only nuclear tests ever carried out.) I thought my letter would have appeared a day or two later but it didn't and I began to think I'd better forget about the whole thing. Then I received a phone call from a reporter named David Livingstone who said the *Daily Record* would like to do an article on me. I immediately agreed to this proposal despite the fact I'd never been interviewed before in my life.

An article appeared in the newspaper on 24 November and suddenly other letters began to pour into the paper's offices, from ex-servicemen who'd been stationed on Christmas Island at that time. One of these early letters which was passed on to me came from a man called Philip Munn who lived in nearby East Kilbride. Philip was suffering from leukaemia, a condition he sincerely believed was attributable to his service on the island. I was astonished to find lots of other cases involving ex-servicemen who went through physical and mental torture on a daily basis without any substantial help from the authorities. To make matters worse, it soon became clear that the military establishment refused to believe these veterans when they claimed they'd fallen into ill-health because they'd taken part in the nuclear test programme. Suddenly, without realising it, I was the focus for the veterans' cause and men from all over the United Kingdom began to write to me with their own stories of life before, during and after Christmas Island.

The media know the makings of a good story when they see it and I was pleasantly surprised when I was invited to go on BBC Radio Scotland. I journeyed up to the BBC headquarters in Queen Margaret Drive in Glasgow where the interview was being taped and edited before being finally aired throughout the country. The interview started well enough then suddenly the chap suggested that my claims bordered on the "eccentric". I was annoyed and asked him to justify the use of this adjective. He shrugged his shoulders and we started the interview again. This was to be a foretaste of what was to come in later years.

In the space of a few weeks I received hundreds and hundreds of letters. One man from England said he felt his medical records were, like mine, incomplete and he was sure they'd been tampered with since his return. The BBC TV programme *Nationwide* had a chat with me and decided to highlight our claims in one of their December 1982 editions.

A few weeks later *Nationwide* broadcast an edition about our cause, illustrating it with old press clippings with headlines like "JURY REJECT RADIATION AS DEATH CAUSE", "ATOM BOMB CAUSED DEATH SAYS LEGION", "A-BOMB ISLE SAPPER DIED SIX MONTHS AFTER BLAST" and "H-BOMB ISLE OFFICER DIES OF LEUKAEMIA – NAVY DENIAL". This showed that our claims had some historical integrity and that couldn't be dismissed as the paranoid ravings of a bunch of old soldiers. The programme also referred to the nuclear bomb tests which the United States had carried out in the 1940–62 period, something which I was just beginning to educate myself about. The public were informed about the basic medical effects which radiation can induce in human beings. Strong doses, for example, can lead to immediate death. Lower doses can cause leukaemia, lymphatic cancers, genetic disorders and sterility.

Dr Hugh Evans, a radiation protection officer from Imperial College, was interviewed during one of the *Nationwide* episodes. When asked questions relating to the bomb trials on Christmas Island he commented:

> . . . All these weapons were air-bursts, there was no fall-out at all on the island and when you work out the actual doses they received, they couldn't have been nearer than fifteen miles, incidentally even the scientists were that distance and the non-essential personnel were about twenty-four miles. Even at fifteen miles the actual dosage during the detonation itself, which is all they could receive, would be something like, oh . . . several million times less than they would receive if they had a weekend in Cornwall.

In light of the rain which suddenly fell on my bulldozer immediately after the 28 April bomb trial and taking into consideration the letter from the Shackelton pilot, I considered Dr Evan's comments to be at best, bizarre and at worst, dangerously ill-informed. During the same interview, Dr Evans casually produced a little "dosimeter" which caught the eye of the programme's presenter:

> *Interviewer:* You've got this small indicator, now that . . . would the men have been wearing something like that near this area?
> *Dr Evans:* Anyone seriously running any risk at all of exposure to radiation would have worn a thing like this, this is a

film-badge, a small device that looks simple, but it's a very sophisticated thing really which actually measures the radiation dose . . . .

Needless to say, I'd never seen this piece of equipment in my life and, as I mentioned earlier, I never clapped eyes on one during my 351-day stay on Christmas Island. But, as I watched Dr Evans holding the little dosimeter, I wondered if I could possibly be mistaken – perhaps I *had* been given a film-badge but I'd just forgotten about it during the excitement of the tests?

My doubts were erased with the next episode of *Nationwide* for, as presenter Hugh Scully opened the programme, he said:

> Since the programme we've had a very large response, calls and letters have come in from many parts of the country from ex-servicemen and relatives of men who served in the area. Many of these calls and letters have disagreed with the official version of events which is that the tests were quite safe. In particular, a lot of those who got in touch with us say that many of the servicemen involved with the tests were not issued with badges designed to show how much radiation they'd received . . . .

After I heard this I knew that I was on to something. Within a few days, and with the help of the *Nationwide* team, I was able to contact some of the other servicemen who had featured on the programme. Over a few months I began to compare notes with men like Philip Munn, Eddie Eagan and Tom Armstrong from England. I spoke to a Mr David Gee, a union official, who put me in touch with Dr Alice Stewart from the Social Medicine Department of Birmingham University. A day or two later I made an appointment with Dr Stewart and, together with Philip Munn, Tom Armstrong, Ron Tarran and Terry and Rita Dale, I travelled down to Birmingham. A London-based solicitor named Mr Mark Mildred was drafted in to advise us on any important legal matters arising from our discussions. After going over all our details we decided to send out a rudimentary questionnaire to all the servicemen who had contacted *Nationwide* to be sent back for Dr Stewart to study. Our initiative was suddenly gathering speed and everyone realised the urgent need for a central body which could effectively co-ordinate everything. Thus, on 5 May 1983 we formed the British Nuclear Test Veterans Association and I was voted in as the Chairman.

During the drive back up to Scotland I contemplated my future with the BNTVA. I was full of doubts and I wasn't sure just how long our campaign would last. Everything was happening at a furious pace and I wondered whether I could sustain that kind of momentum in the future. When I finally arrived home in Dunoon I rang *Nationwide* to tell them about the new association for ex-servicemen and they broadcast all the details about the BNTVA a few days later. I received over two hundred phone-calls within the next three days from men wanting to join. The long hard slog had started.

Chapter Five

OVER A PERIOD of a few months I received hundreds of letters from all over the country. I couldn't believe that all these letters came from ex-servicemen, widows and families of ex-servicemen who wanted to join the association. They all agreed with our main aim which was to ask the authorities to recognise the possible damage inflicted on the personnel who participated in all the British nuclear tests. After a few days of sorting through the mail I realised I had enough members to set up branches throughout the country. I remember writing to Ken Taylor in London and asking him to organise the very first branch of the BNTVA in his area. Ken had worked in the Port Camp cookhouse on Christmas Island during the bomb tests and he remembered me standing in the queues waiting for my lunch with all the other men. It was nice to have him back on my side after all these years. Branches were formed in the Midlands, North-East and North-West of England and the members represented every rank and regiment that you could possibly imagine. We decided that we needed a patron for the organisation, a well-known individual who would publicly support our cause. I wrote to Patricia Phoenix who was known throughout the land as Elsie Tanner of *Coronation Street*. A few days later a handwritten reply arrived on my doorstep:

Dear Mr McGinley,
    Thank you for your letter which I found deeply moving. I am honoured and proud to be asked to become the Patron of your most just and worthy cause and I shall do whatever I can, whenever I can to draw the Public and Parliament's notice as the justice of your cause . . . Please keep me informed as to how and when I can help, thank you for honouring me so,

Sincerely,
Pat Phoenix

Me, looking ckeeky at eight

B.I.S.N. Co's m.s. 'DUNERA' 12,615 ton

TT Dunera, the ship on which I sailed to Christmas Island

Wammi, a Fijian soldier, and I on Christmas Island in 1958

Alan "Tiny" Robinson, as he was when I first met him

Preparing for the Cup final on Christmas Island: "Tiny" Robinson is fourth from the left with me, second from the right – examining my feet

28 April 1958: my first megaton bomb (note the debris at the base of the mushroom stalk)

Our accommodation before and after the blast of 28 April 1958

The injury that didn't happen – according to government officials, of course

Tom Birch as he was in 1958

Wee Frank, on the beach at Christmas Island

On the campaign trail: in Japan

with STAG

with American atomic veteran, Anthony Guarisco

Me with the brave Kiev fireman post Chernobyl, 1986

The British Nuclear Test Veterans Association, 1990

My wife Alice, daughter Louise and myself, today

It was during the first few months of the association that I received a phone-call from an ex-officer who had served on Christmas Island. The gentleman introduced himself to me in a very polite upper-crust accent and said he was due to go into hospital for an operation on a cancerous tumour which he'd been suffering from for a number of years.

"I might not come out of the hospital alive," he suddenly remarked.

I was shell-shocked. I couldn't imagine that I was talking to a man who might die within the space of a week. I asked him if there was anything I could do which might help him.

"Yes," he replied calmly, "that's why I rang you, Mr McGinley."

There was a moment's silence then the voice on the other end of the line said:

"If I should die, Mr McGinley, then please make sure that you get the bastards for me . . . ."

This ex-officer died in hospital a week later. His words have never left me and the feeling with which he said them is part of the BNTVA's foundation.

Only a week later I found out that my friend, Tony Crampsey from Johnstone, had also died from cancer. Tony had been in ill-health ever since his return from Christmas Island and the news of his death hit me hard.

The association started to attract enormous attention from all sections of the media throughout the United Kingdom and journalists watched programmes like *Nationwide* before contacting me to obtain more information. Others had read some interesting articles which had appeared in the medical press, especially *The Lancet* which had published two lengthy letters referring to our case. The letters came from a whole body of qualified and respected experts and they read as follows:

Sir,

In December, 1982, the BBC television programme "Nationwide" initiated a follow-up of men who had been involved in nuclear weapons testing in the South Pacific by inviting first-hand accounts from viewers. The programme also enlisted our help with the statistical analysis of reported illnesses and deaths.

The South Pacific tests – whose local base was Christmas Island – overlapped in time with other weapons tests. Thus, there were twelve tests in Western and South Australia between 1952 and 1957, and nine South Pacific tests between May, 1957, and November, 1958. The follow-up of the South

Pacific population is far from complete but already there is evidence of an abnormally high incidence of leukaemia and other reticuloendothelial system (RES) neoplasms . . . .

Department of Social Medicine
University of Birmingham
Birmingham B15 2TH

[Signed]
E. G. Knox
Tom Sorahan
Alice Stewart

Sir,

The figures presented in the above letter by Professor Knox, Dr Sorahan and Dr Stewart, which refer to the men involved in the South Pacific tests during 1957-58, even on the most conservative of estimates reveal a subsequent incidence of RES malignancies greatly in excess of the numbers expected on the basis of the relevant population statistics when analysed strictly in accordance with life-table methods. While, as Knox and his colleagues suggest, there may be causes other than radiation for the excess RES malignancies, the reported incidence of cataract, virtually unknown as a spontaneous occurrence among young men, is a strong indication that some of those involved had received radiation greatly in excess of a safe dose.

The servicemen present at the nuclear test explosions constitute a uniquely large sample of healthy young men who were at risk of exposure to ionising radiation and among whom there now appears to be evidence of radiation related effects. To examine as fully as possible their subsequent medical histories, access to a complete nominal roll of the total group of exposed persons is required, together with full disclosure of what is known about radiation exposure of men on duty during these tests. We urge that an independent academic body be asked to conduct a full investigation into the morbidity, mortality and perhaps genetic effects in these men, and given the means to do so.

Sutton, Surrey
St Mary's Hospital, London
London
Welsh National School of Medicine, Cardiff
St Bart's Hospital Medical School, Medical College, London
London
Middlesex Hospital Medical School, London

[Signed]
J. W. Boag
J. Fielding
John H. Humphrey
Allan Jacobs

Patricia Lindop
Joseph Rotblat

James A. Thompson

Admittedly, some of these early results used statistics which were later proved to be incorrect but the broad basis of their findings are still, in my view, valid today. But the publication of the letters also gave our association a respectable scientific foundation and presented our case to a much wider and potentially more powerful section of the public.

Our campaign continued to go from strength to strength, especially after our discovery of some highly sensitive documents in the Public Records Office at Kew in London. The association's London representative, Ken Taylor, managed to dig out some horrific papers which related to the United Kingdom's nuclear test programme. This was a feat in itself for Ken since, ironically, he suffered from cataracts in his eyes. This was one of the diseases associated with exposure to radiation and it was referred to by Boag *et al* in the second of the two letters from *The Lancet* printed above. Many of the documents which Ken managed to unearth were marked "TOP SECRET" or "RESTRICTED CIRCULATION", and they sketch out the precarious nature of the United Kingdom's nuclear weapons trials from start to finish. If the reader takes these papers by themselves then they don't appear to mean much but if they are placed into their true historical context and read alongside the personal accounts of some men who were involved in the nuclear test programme, then their significance increases ten-fold.

It took the association a few difficult months, filled with lots of hard academic grafting, to assemble a catalogue of damning evidence which we hoped the British military establishment could not ignore. On examining it we soon realised that the Ministry of Defence and the scientists who were involved in the early planning stages of the bomb trials were often under enormous pressure to complete experiments and deliver the results as quickly as possible. The documents gave the impression that safety was often compromised for speed during this important process. Take, for example, a letter I received from a gentleman who worked at a Ministry of Defence establishment near Oxford. This man was only twenty-three years old when he participated in the highly sensitive and extremely dangerous production of the trigger devices used to detonate the atomic bombs. The letter explained that the young man handled a rare substance called Polonium-210 which was used in the their manufacturing process. This substance was not used by the USA since it was regarded as being far too dangerous and unpredictable, yet here was a twenty-three-old coming into contact with it on a daily basis. (Polonium would receive a certain notoriety in later years when it was revealed that it was contained in the lethal radioactive cloud which was released over the south-east of England in the aftermath of the infamous Windscale disaster in 1957. Some experts have claimed that as many as half of the projected cancers following this incident will be due to innocent members of the population coming into contact with Polonium-210.) The letter which I received contained some startling information about the conditions which many civilian research workers had to work under in the build-up to the early atomic tests. It states:

> I started work at Harwell under the Ministry of Supply in October 1951. For the next 13 months I was involved in the research, development and finally production of the Polonium trigger for Britain's atomic bomb which was tested at Monte Bello or Xmas Island in 1952.
>
> Polomium 210 is a powerful alpha emitter with a half life of 139 days and in those early days lab workers had little or no protection from radiation. The lab in which I worked was originally scheduled for research only with actual full scale production to be undertaken in the Windscale factory. In the event, Windscale was not ready in time to produce factory quantities of Polonium hence Harwell personnel had to handle vast, almost unheard of quantities even by today's standards of up to 30 Curies of Polonium. The material was completely unpredictable and almost uncontainable. One memorable night when entering the lab at dusk we solved the problem of some missing Polonium. There it was glowing eerily on the walls of the lab. Believe it or not it was removed by washing the entire lab (about 500 sq. feet of floor area plus walls and ceiling) with Kleenex tissues soaked in acid. Such were the conditions in which we worked. Protection was from rubber gloves and lightweight hoods fed with compressed air.
>
> At one stage we became contaminated so regularly that we had to oxidize the skin on our hands with Potassium Permanganate and in so doing we moved most of the radioactive material.
>
> Regular checks of blood and urine were made and we wore film monitors on wrists and lapels. Theoretical dose limits were fixed but were often exceeded. No other workers were available and Winston Churchill in personal charge of the operation had decreed that the bomb had to be tested on the fixed date.
>
> When production of Polonium ceased I went to the army for three years before returning to Harwell to work on the recovery of Polonium residues from the electro-magnetic separator. During this latter period I was exposed to the

hazards previously encountered but nothing like the scale of Polonium.

For the past 18 to 20 years or so, I have never felt really 100% fit and well. Most doctors over the period have put my symptoms down to sinus trouble and I have accepted this. Within the last couple of years however I became fed up with my "sinus" problem and requested specialist advice which was readily available. Exhaustive tests have proved that my problems of headaches, heavy perspiration, weight increase and dreadful lack of energy can be attributed to an underactive thyroid. I am now on pills for the rest of my life and have been exempted from all prescription charges.

The contents of this letter are startling and to a large extent speak for themselves. What scared me even more, however, was the fact that the authorities were apparently well aware of the dangers which could result from workers handling such radioactive substances. One of the first documents which we found in the PRO related to a meeting which took place in Conference Room "A", Cabinet Office, Great George Street, London SW1, on Thursday, 24 July 1947, at 2.30 p.m. The document reads as follows:

The committee had before them (a) the draft Radioactive Substances Bill . . .

MR. REED stated that the main object of the Bill was to protect from the effects of radioactive materials and hard X-rays (1) workers in places not covered by the Factories Act, such as university laboratories, hospitals and transport facilities; (2) patients under treatment; also to prevent dangerous general contamination by radioactive effluents from factories, etc . . .

SIR ERNEST ROCK CARLING agreed that there were many chances of undesirable exposures to radiation in hospitals and research laboratories. The resulting injuries were frequently not traced to radiation since there might be a lag of months or years before the effects were manifest. Carelessness might also have serious genetic effects on the population, resulting in sterility or mutations. These effects were probably cumulative.

DR. MITCHELL agreed with this, pointing out that occupational illnesses due to exposure to radiations might have a latent period of as much as ten years, free from all clinical symptoms. The genetic effects were caused by lower intensities of radiation.

All the members of the association who clapped eyes on this document were shocked. Previously, we never thought for one moment that we had been deliberately neglected by the authorities who had known all along what the long-term effects on our health would be. But this appeared to have been the case. The American Government had held its own nuclear tests long before the British got around to building either the A- or H-bombs. From documents which came slowly but surely out of Kew it was clear that a relatively free flow of information was exchanged between both sides of the Atlantic. In the wake of the US's early tests with megaton weapons, the UK scientists had plenty of up-to-date information about the biological effects of radiation on human beings in a combat situation. This is particularly clear when one reads a document which dates back to July 1953. This report contains the minutes of a meeting which was held at the Atomic Energy Research Establishment (AERE) which is located at Harwell in Oxfordshire. Various important scientific and military personnel attended the meeting, notable amongst whom was Dr Karl Morgan from the Oak Ridge Establishment in Tennessee, USA. In the third paragraph of this document the reader is informed:

> Dr Karl Morgan in reply to a question by Dr Williams stated that in practice for an atomic trial the ratio of betas to gammas was 100 or more. He stated that erythrma had occurred. He said that he hoped we would not follow too closely what they had done and would profit by the mistakes that they had made. He also stated that the American Handbook on the effects of Atomic Weapons contained so many inaccuracies that it would be wise not to follow this handbook . . . in actual practice, he said that a limited area of skin, such as the face and hands, could not be taken in planning procedures since often men strip to the waist, wear little or no clothing and that it would be wise to plan for total body radiation and not to include a factor for limited areas of skin. He assumed that the men would be wearing footwear with thick soles.

This document really speaks for itself. The Americans had carried out their own experimental tests using their own soldiers. The data had been collected afterwards and it was now being passed on to the UK. Therefore, Britain knew what the effects of radiation on the health of its men would be . . . yet they still went ahead. I was really disgusted when I realised all this. So much for the old standby line "they didn't know what they were doing", eh? Another report from 1947, for example, highlights the genetic damage which can be wrought on anyone being irradiated:

MEDICAL RESEARCH COUNCIL
Genetic Effects of Irradiation with Reference to Man.
by D. G. Catcheside
(2) All quantitive experiments show that even the smallest doses
of radiation produce a genetic effect, there being no dose below
which no genetic effect is induced.

I read this in amazement. I knew that radiation might have played a
part in my low sperm count but I never thought that this information
had been available *prior* to us young men participating in the United
Kingdom nuclear bomb trials. But, after some more research, I came
to realise that selected top military personnel had been briefed
before they went to Christmas Island about the possible dangers
from exposure to radiation before the tests. The author of the
Christmas Island Story, an article which appeared in the newspaper
we received whilst we were stationed on the island, was a surgeon
called Commander P. D. G. Pugh, RN. In his lengthy and rather
boring piece he recounts the following astonishing details:

> I do not propose to delve too deeply into the events which
> preceded our departure from the United Kingdom. It was
> a particularly busy period. As "Warrior" was to be in the
> forward area, I had to consider the procedures and investigation
> to be carried out in the highly unlikely event of casualties
> being incurred. In this connexion, visits were paid to the
> R.N. Medical School and the Atomic Weapons Research
> Establishment (A.W.R.E.) at Aldermaston, where I discussed
> these matters with Doctor Lynch the Principal Medical Officer
> and other officers of the establishment. From all I received the
> utmost co-operation, and most helpful advice. I also visited
> Harwell where I first made the acquaintance of Air Commander
> Wilson, the personal advisor to the Task Force Commander on
> matters relating to radiation, and his assistant, Squadron Leader
> Sturrock.
>
> As a result of these discussions proposals were drafted and
> finally approved to standardise throughout the squadron, both
> the investigations and treatment of any casualties. As so little
> is known about radiation injuries, stress was laid on the
> importance of keeping a detailed record of such patients and
> ideal investigations were listed. It was clear, however, that
> the circumstances could be such that only a limited number
> of these procedures could be carried out. In such an event,
> a daily blood smear, and urine collection (for forwarding to
> A.W.R.E.) were selected as the most valuable and simple

of the available investigations. Facilities for coloured clinical photography were also made available aboard "Warrior".

A routine for the treatment of radiation injuries, thermal burns, and mechanical trauma was laid down, it being proposed to deal with all major trauma in the operating theatre in "Warrior".

This information led me to the conclusion that some of the medical/ scientific personnel were really treating the whole series of bomb trials as nothing more than an ideal opportunity to gather data on the medical effects of fall-out on humans. Even if you give them the benefit of the doubt and stop short of accusing them of deliberately exposing men to radiation as part of an experiment, you must still agree that they would be quite prepared to gobble up every scrap of information which came their way on the effects of radiation if they happened to find themselves in the fortunate position of witnessing an accident. Why else would contingency plans be made to relay results of daily blood-smears and urine samples back to AWRE in the United Kingdom and for "coloured clinical photography" facilities to be available on board ships?

As more documents came to light I grew increasingly angry and I kept asking myself the same old question over and over again; why had all the ordinary soldiers not been told about the dangers of radiation? We had always assumed, indeed been told, that there was no risk involved in taking part in the tests. The answer to this question came when I read another document obtained about two months after the BNTVA was founded. I remember leaving my house one morning to catch a flight to London when the postman suddenly arrived with a large brown envelope for me. I opened it quickly and found a "TOP SECRET" paper inside with a small typed note. The anonymous sender briefly said something to the effect that this document would help the association and I would be sent more in due course. As it turned out I wasn't sent any more but I needn't have worried for this document proved enough to capture the attention of the nation's media. The report is dated 20 May 1953 and it reads:

CHIEFS OF STAFF COMMITTEE
ATOMIC WEAPONS TRIALS
Report by the Defence Research Policy Committee

Many of these tests are of the highest importance to departments, since on their results depend the design of equipment, changes

in organisation and administration and information on effects of
various types of atomic explosions on ships and their contents
and equipment. Although some information is available from
the earliest American trials and from HURRICAINE there is
much to be learned before essential decisions can be taken on
the design of future ships. *The army must discover the detailed
effects of various types of explosion on equipment, stores and men
with and without various types of protection.* [Author's italics]

In other words, this document was saying that we had all been used by
the authorities in order to gain valuable scientific data for research into
the effects of radiation on human beings. And the earlier documents
prove that the authorities knew what the dangers to our health would
be. The illness and the death which had eaten its way into the lives
of my friends and which had caused me so much pain and anguish
over the years was the direct result of my presence on Christmas Island
during the bomb tests. The evidence which I had before me proved
that we had all been used.

This document from 1953 was soon picked up by journalists and
politicians. The association had already harnessed cross-party support
from the latter group. Mr Winston Churchill MP, Mr David Alton MP
and Jack Ashley MP were three of our most enthusiastic Parliamentary
supporters. On 12 March 1984, Mr David Alton MP spoke on the floor
of the House of Commons about the British Nuclear Test Veterans
Association:

> I am sorry that the Minister of State who has just replied to the
> previous debate should have the invidious task of replying also
> to this one. He could be forgiven for a sense of déjà vu, since
> last July, in another Consolidated Fund Bill debate on this same
> subject – atomic explosions in the South Pacific in the 1950s –
> he also drew the short straw.
>
> I make no apology for having sought to raise this important
> issue again. I want to return to some of the questions that I put
> to the Minister last July. First, I want to press him on orders
> which were issued to our servicemen and the conditions which
> prevailed during those tests . . .
>
> The Minister will have received from me a copy of the report
> of the Defence Research Policy Committee, circulated on 20 May
> 1953, which has been made available through the Public Record
> Office under the 30-year rule. This document was written in
> May 1953, six months after Britain's first nuclear explosion off

the coast of the Monte Bello islands in Western Australian. In October 1953 Britain tested two more devices at Emu Field in South Australia. This is among the first official records to be released on the atomic bomb tests. It says:

"Many of these tests are of the highest importance to departments, since on their results depend the design of equipment, changes in organisation and administration, and offensive and defensive tactics."

The report says that the Navy required information on the effects of various types of atomic explosions on ships, their contents and equipment. The RAF similarly wanted information on the effects of explosions on airfields, submarine bases and the oil industry.

Undoubtedly the most disquieting and disturbing part of the report refers to the Army's requirements. This 1953 report says:

"The Army must discover the detailed effects of various types of explosion on equipment, stores and men, with and without various forms of protection."

In a concise and tightly written report, there is no equivocation or ambiguity. Men were to be used as human guinea pigs – not dummies or instruments. Men were to be deliberately exposed to the effects of radiation, with and without protective clothing. It was to be a glorified scientific experiment.

It says something for, at best, the woeful ignorance, and, at worst, the callous indifference of those who issued those orders that, in the Army's book, equipment and stores appear to rank higher than men in this bizarre order of merit . . . .

In 1982, one year before the British Nuclear Test Veterans Association had been formed, Britain witnessed unparalleled scenes of national fervour in the aftermath of the Falklands conflict. When I saw the way those young servicemen were honoured by the Conservative government I was sure we would be treated fairly. So, when the government announced in 1983 that it would commission an independent body to carry out a study to look into the association's claims, I started to feel that at last we might be getting somewhere.

I think I can safely say that all the veterans expected the government to award the contract for the study to a truly independent expert body. Boag *et al* had suggested as much in their letter to *The Lancet* when they said:

> We urge that an independent academic body be asked to conduct a full investigation into the morbidity, mortality and perhaps genetic effects in these men, and given the means to do so.

However, the government decided to award the contract to the National Radiological Protection Board.

As soon as this announcement was made I began to receive phone-calls from highly qualified and expert individuals who felt that we'd been short-changed. I was told that the NRPB was far from independent in the true sense of the word and that it was more or less the government's right hand when it came to all matters nuclear. I soon learned that this organisation, which had been established in 1970, had something of a reputation for taking decisions which never harmed the nuclear power industry in Britain. A prime example of this laissez faire approach was the 1983 report which the NRPB wrote concerning the 1957 Windscale disaster. This report included estimates of the number of cancers which could result from the accident but it made no mention of the likely effects of Polonium-210 which was also released into the atmosphere. This is the same Polonium-210 which was mentioned earlier in a letter I received from a former employee of the United Kingdom Atomic Energy Authority which was based at Harwell. Journalists and scientific commentators soon picked up this startling flaw in the NRPB's Windscale report, pointing out that the Polonium-210 issue should have been addressed because the substance is widely acknowledged as being one of the most carcinogenic. Intense criticism of this omission forced the NRPB to add another section to its Windscale report which dealt with the Polonium-210 controversy and revise its estimates concerning the number of cancers caused by the 1957 fire.

By 12 March 1984 the doubts about the impartiality had reached the House of Commons. Mr David Alton MP referred to the problem during a Commons' debate on the atomic tests:

> The Minister will also recall that I expressed doubts about the suitability of the National Radiological Protection Board to conduct the survey. I suggested that it was a case of the watchdog being too closely identified with the burglar. The view of the Joint Committee on the Medical Effects of Nuclear Weapons is contained in a letter which reached me today. It states:
> "The National Radiological Protection Board's expertise is in monitoring radiation exposure, not in carrying out health surveys such as the one entrusted to it by the Secretary of State for Defence. Indeed, the study was to have been headed by a physicist [who has since

died] not a medical epidemiologist. An investigation of
the complexity of the one to be undertaken could only
be carried out satisfactorily by persons suitably trained.
At the very outset of the NRPB's study, therefore,
sceptics may find some confirmation for doubts aroused
by the Government's entrusting an investigation of its own
liability to a government body. The choice is surprising
in view of the fact that there are at least five university
departments which would be sure to carry out the study
with an academic impartiality which could not reasonably
be questioned."

Does the Minister fully realise the high scientific standards
that will be expected of the study and the care with which
data will not just need to be collected if the results are to
be seen clearly by the medical profession, the patients and
bereaved relatives to have been reached by objective and
impartial processes?

Will the Minister confirm that every step will be taken to
ensure that the greatest scientific rigour is brought to bear?
Many bereaved relatives see the long drawn-out nature of
the survey as a way to try and dampen opposition and fob
off people . . .

Mr Gavin Strang, MP for Edinburgh East, also made a valuable
contribution to the same debate:

I congratulate the Hon. Member for Liverpool, Mosley Hill [Mr
Alton] on raising an important subject which, I am sure both
he and the Minister agree, must be properly investigated and
debated in the coming months . . .
The House will be well aware of the history of these
developments and of the famous letter published by Dr. Alice
Stewart and her colleagues in "The Lancet" last April. I also pay
tribute to the tremendous work being done by the British Nuclear
Test Veterans Association and its Chairman, Ken McGinley, in
seeking, first, to locate and identify as many people as possible
who participated in the tests and, secondly, to focus public
attention on this issue of immense importance not only to them
and their families but to the country generally . . . I agree with
the Hon. Member for Mosley Hill that it would have been far
better to have the survey carried out by an independent group. I
in no way seek to criticise the National Radiological Protection
Board, but, with respect, it would have been much better if
university departments or even the Royal Society of Scientists

had been involved in carrying out the study. I hope that at this late stage the Government will not rule out looking into that again.

But the Government did not change its mind over its decision to commission the NRPB to carry out a study into the veterans' health. I wasn't sure what to do at the time. On the one hand I realised that many people, including myself, had strong misgivings about the impartiality of the NRPB. On the other hand, I knew that this might be our one and only chance to obtain a relatively fair hearing. I thought that I could tip the balance in our favour by co-operating as fully as possible with the NRPB during their investigations. I sent them every shred of evidence that I had on the veterans and they were given every single medical questionnaire which I'd received from men who had participated in the bomb trials. I even agreed to pay a visit to the NRPB's headquarters at Didcot in Oxfordshire in late 1983. Accompanying me on this trip were the association's legal advisor, Mr Mark Mildred, and a few members of the association, including Mike Doyle and Peter Fletcher.

The headquarters were located in the middle of nowhere and resembled a rather bland hi-tech factory. Security inside was tight and as you walked through the front door you were issued with a special identity card. We were greeted by some personnel from the NRPB and were taken for a working lunch which consisted of cans of beer and sandwiches in the staff canteen. I felt rather uncomfortable and had the awful feeling that we were being slightly patronised by our hosts who thought we weren't worthy of a decent meal in a more private location. Under these difficult circumstances the conversation was somewhat strained yet we all did out best to try and be as optimistic as possible. But, as each minute passed by, I got the impression that the NRPB were as much in the dark about the whole issue as we had been at the beginning of our campaign. They told us that they were compiling their statistical information from the Ministry of Defence's source known as the Blue Book. This reputedly held the names of all the known military and civilian units which were involved in the testing of nuclear weapons. Although they spoke about the Blue Book with a certain amount of enthusiasm, I knew deep down that they weren't too sure about the accuracy of its contents. In fact, when they mentioned HMS Resolution, the camp I was stationed at on Christmas Island, they seemed to think that it was a ship! So much for all the researchers who were milling around us.

As our party was preparing to leave the NRPB building I asked one of the staff if I could possibly see a dosimeter since I'd heard a lot about them but I'd never actually seen one. I was led through a maze of corridors and shown into a small room where an attractive young lady in a white overall was working.

"Could I have a dosimeter for Mr McGinley please?" the NRPB gentleman asked her.

"Use one off of that board," she said without lifting her head.

A large board holding lots of little badges stood nearby. The NRPB chap lifted a little dosimeter down and turned to the girl:

"Is this one okay?" he asked.

"Oh no," she chirped, "that's an old obsolete model from nine months ago and that kind are out of date now."

When the assistant said the dosimeter was "obsolete and out of date" despite it being only nine months old, I just looked around me in silence. No member of our party said a word, we didn't have to. The message I was trying to get across slowly sunk in. If these dosimeters were considered old-fashioned and had been surpassed by more sophisticated devices, then how efficient were the devices we were supposed to have been given thirty years before? Surely any readings from such basic equipment which had a three-decade vintage could not be used in any modern study which dealt with the highly complex effects of exposure to radiation? No answer was required and we left the NRPB's building the same way we had arrived – with a feeling of scepticism.

Immediately after the BNTVA was founded in May 1983, we received a letter from the United States. On opening it we discovered it was sent by the American Atomic Veterans' Association who were about to hold a large conference in New York city and the sender of the letter, Mr Anthony Guarisco, invited two members of our association over to attend. A witness to some of the world's first nuclear explosions, Anthony Guarisco, sixty-three, served in the United States Navy in the Pacific during the Second World War. Following the war, Seaman First Class Guarisco was stationed at Bikini Atoll. There, at the age of nineteen, he took part in "Operation Crossroads", witnessing the atomic tests "ABLE" and "BAKER". He spent sixty-seven days at "Ground Zero" in the contaminated lagoon, experiencing the acute symptoms of radiation exposure following the second blast. Honourably discharged in 1947, Mr Guarisco married in 1955. He then began a plumbing contracting business in Los

Angeles, but was plagued by a series of lung, urological, bone and heart disorders. Disabled, he joined the National Association of Atomic Veterans in the United States in 1981. The following year, the Veterans' Administration rejected his disability claim. But by 1983, the same year the BNTVA was founded, Anthony was the Director of the International Alliance of Atomic Veterans and it was in this capacity that he was inviting two members of our association over to the United States. I was tied up with lots of other engagements and important matters in the United Kingdom so I was delighted to see Phil Munn and another member journey over on our behalf. They both had a wonderful week in the United States and came home full of praise for Anthony Guarisco and his lovely wife Mary.

A year later, in 1984, I received a call from Anthony asking me to travel over to the USA to participate in a five-week tour of the country with the International Alliance of Atomic Veterans. Our expenses for this trip, he explained, would be met by Greenpeace. I decided to take up this invitation along with an another BNTVA member, Mr John Price. The association was able to give us a hundred pounds each towards any incidental expenses we might need to meet during our trip. I left from Gatwick Airport in London on a Virgin Airline flight to JFK, New York. I used much of the time during the flight to do some research into the history of the atomic test issue in the United States. The material I had in front of me revealed some startling facts.

America's very first atomic bomb, commonly referred to as the "Trinity" shot, was detonated in the atmosphere above New Mexico on 16 July 1945. A few weeks later, two other atomic explosions took place in the form of war bombs in Hiroshima and Nagasaki. Realising the military potential of this new weapon, the US Government gave the go-ahead for two atomic testing grounds to be sighted on the Bikini and Eniwetok atolls in the Marshall Islands. These locations were the test sights for a further five atomic explosions in the years prior to 1950. The year 1950 proved to be something of a turning point in the US nuclear weapons-testing programme. The war in Korea during that year meant the government had to rethink its atomic-test programme, taking into consideration the possibility that the tests might be undertaken within the borders of the USA. All the tests were to be carried out under the direct authority of the country's Atomic Energy Commission (AEC). Even at this early stage the AEC was well aware of the dangers to the military and general population who were in and around the test-site area. Despite this damaging knowledge, however, the AEC still went ahead to recommend that the US Government consider its short-list of possible testing sights within the USA. Clearly, at the outset of the country's nuclear-test programme, the advancement of the nation's military capability was being given precedence over the safety of its inhabitants. This "rush" of research at the cost of human life in the United States bears a striking resemblance to the Polonium-210 situation described in the letter I mentioned earlier and the crude conditions in the laboratory in Harwell, in the UK.

On 12 December 1950, following the AEC's formal recommendations, President Harry S. Truman issued the order establishing a continental nuclear testing site. The area chosen as the US mainland test site was the Las Vegas-Tonopah Bombing and Gunnery Range, a government-owned piece of land north of Las Vegas, Nevada. This site became known as The Nevada Proving Ground or, as it was subsequently labelled, the Nevada Test Site. A month later the first nuclear test was carried out using this site. From January 1951 through October 1958 some 121 atmospheric tests were conducted at the Nevada Test Site. The tests were shelved between October 1959 and September 1961 as a result of the voluntary moratorium which was agreed between the United States and the Soviet Union. Between September 1961, when this agreement expired, and August 1963, a further 102 atmospheric tests took place in Nevada. The atmospheric tests eventually ceased completely after President John F. Kennedy signed the Limited Nuclear Test Ban Treaty on 5 August 1963 along with the Soviet Union and the United Kingdom.

Most of the US atmospheric tests involved "surface-bursts", which produced enormous amounts of radioactive fall-out after the devices had been detonated. Thousands of innocent young American soldiers were led into the area known as "Ground Zero" where there were deplorable levels of radioactive contamination. Many were watched closely by scientists who were openly carrying out experiments into the psychological effects which nuclear blasts had on military performance. These troops were issued with rudimentary film-badges which were supposed to keep them out of any danger. In reality, the badges were usually binned after the exercises were completed and no account was taken of the possibility that the young soldiers might have inhaled the radioactive dust which coated the desert after the atomic blasts. This dust came down to earth in the surrounding areas which were populated with livestock and, in many cases, human beings. I read an official US Government report which looked into the damage which was done by this radioactive dust and into the early attempts to cover up the issue by the AEC. This document, entitled "'THE FORGOTTEN GUINEA PIGS' – A REPORT ON HEALTH EFFECTS OF LOW-LEVEL RADIATION SUSTAINED AS A RESULT OF THE NUCLEAR WEAPONS TESTING PROGRAM CONDUCTED BY THE UNITED STATES GOVERNMENT", reads:

> The two tests which contributed the greatest amounts of fallout to areas where sheep were known to be grazing were the 24.4-kiloton "Nancy" shot fired on a 300-foot tower on May 19, 1953. At the time of these two test shots, 11,710 sheep were grazing in an area from 40 miles north to 160 miles east of the test site. Of these sheep, 1,420 lambing ewes (12.1%) and 2,970 new lambs (25.4%) died during the spring and summer of 1953.

This information only came to light in this 1980 report but back in 1953 some farmers and vets in the area knew that something was far wrong. The concern that these local farmers expressed at the time is documented in considerable detail in the report:

> We were on the trail home from our Nevada range into our Utah range, and I was out on the saddle horse with this herd of sheep just sitting . . . kind of watching the sheep. They were grazing, and these airplanes came over . . . and all at once this bomb dropped . . . .
> I wasn't expecting it . . . it just was an atomic bomb . . . And of course, the cloud came up and drifted over us . . . And, it was a little bit later that day that some of the Army personnel that had four-by-fours and jeeps . . . came through there . . . and they said, "Boy, you guys are really in a hot spot" . . . When they [sheep] started to lamb, we started losing them, and the lambs were born with little legs, kind of pot-bellied. As I remember some of them didn't have any wool, kind of skin instead of wool . . . And we just started losing so many lambs that my father – [who] was alive at that time – just about went crazy. He had never seen anything like it before. Neither had I; neither had anybody else.
>
> (Sheep Rancher)

> I remember going with [Doug Clark] and some of the veterinarians who were doing some autopsies one day, and Doug raised some questions with the team of scientists, one of whom was a colonel

. . . he seemed to be the leading spokesman to kind of press this issue that it couldn't have been radiation. Doug asked him some fairly technical questions about the effects of radiation on internal organs that he'd gotten from other veterinarians. The man, rather than answering the question, called him a dumb sheepman [and] told him he was stupid – he couldn't understand the answer if it was given to him, and for just ten or fifteen minutes, just kind of berated him rather than answer the question.

[And] it was a tough kind of experience for Doug. I remember he left there to go out to his ranch to meet with the loan company to account for what sheep he had left, and within a couple of hours, he was dead from a heart attack. I think that . . . part of the stress that he experienced at that time was that abuse he had received from these officials.

(Iron County Agricultural Agent)

The report goes on to illustrate how the AEC had attempted to deceive the population when they asked questions about the effects of the atomic tests. It states:

The government's concerted effort to discount the evidence correlating the sheep deaths to radioactive fallout clearly was manifested in the AEC's stated policy that the government would not compensate the sheep ranchers for their livestock losses. In furtherance of this policy, the government proceeded to classify all reported evidence to the contrary and disregarded sworn testimony regarding such documentation. Predictably, the sheep ranchers' attempt to litigate their claim for recovery of their losses was thwarted by the government . . . .

As early as 1953, the government was aware of the potential health hazards posed to humans by the internalisation of radionuclides absorbed through the food chain system. Yet, the government failed to take measurements of milk contamination by radioisotopes, upon which to establish internal safety standards, until 1957. Moreover, the government refused to alter the levels subsequently set for internal radiation exposure even after a 1963 scientific report concluded that the government's original assessment of the hazard was substantially underestimated . . . Disregarding personal reports of radiation-related illnesses, which demonstrated potentially higher radiation levels than those actually measured by the government's monitors, the government persistently discounted the possibility of higher radiation doses. Still further, the government publicly espoused the safeness of the atmospheric nuclear testing program as the government also refrained from advertising the health hazards associated with exposure to radioactive fallout.

The Atomic Energy Commission not only prevented potentially damaging evidence from surfacing and therefore undergoing public scrutiny, they also went to considerable lengths to promote vigorously the positive aspects of nuclear testing in Nevada:

> You [the local population] are in a very real sense active participants in the nation's atomic test program. I want you to know that each shot is justified by national or international security and that none will be fired unless there is adequate assurance of public safety. We are grateful for you continued cooperation and your understanding.

This propaganda campaign was enough to fool many residents into really believing that radioactive fall-out was indeed harmless. One woman recalled how she had played with the radioactive dust:

> We liked to play under the trees and shake the fallout onto our heads and our bodies, thinking that we were playing in the snow. I remember writing my name on the car because the fallout dust was so thick . . . . Then I would go home and eat. If my mother caught me as a young child, I would wash my hands; if not, then I would eat with the fallout on my hands.

The woman who told this horrific story was diagnosed in 1958 as having ovarian cancer; later, she developed cancer of the intestines and stomach. In 1970 she developed skin cancer in the vaginal area and, in 1979, leukaemia. She died in March 1983, aged forty-two.

Another gentleman who lived near the Nevada Test Site commented:

> In my own family we have nine cancer victims, beginning with my wife who died of the disease and leukaemia combined; my niece, 5 years old, from leukaemia and cancer; a sister; a sister-in-law; a mother-in-law; an uncle; a grandmother, and two great uncles. I cannot find anywhere in our family records, anywhere as far as we can go, any cancer-related deaths of any nature in our family lines. We have been a very healthy family here.

By 1961, only ten short years after the first Nevada tests were initiated, researchers identified high concentrations, or "clusters", of childhood leukaemia in the communities which were downwind from the nuclear testing site. This earned the local people the macabre title of "the downwinders". More research in later years would substantiate these initial impressions which pointed to the area having a higher than average death-rate from cancer-related illnesses.

Obviously this information shook the hell out of me. Previously, I had only come into contact with individuals who had been irradiated as a direct result of their military service, so it was particularly distressing to hear of innocent families and children suffering as a result of being unwitting witnesses to nuclear tests.

The men I was due to meet when our plane touched down in the United States were a selection of the estimated 235,000 military personnel who had participated in approximately 235 atmospheric nuclear tests between 1945 and 1962. Like the veterans I represented, each of these men had a different tale to tell me, a different horror story of how their lives were permanently changed because they were the first to watch the dawning of our so-called nuclear age.

Our flight arrived in New York and for the first time in nearly thirty years I stepped back on to American soil. The last time I'd been in the country was during that terrible journey back home after the bomb tests on Christmas Island.

John Price and I were greeted by our host for the next five weeks, Anthony Guarisco, and a lovely young woman named Lynn Bylow. Ms Bylow had once been a top fashion model but was forced to give up this profession due to her declining health. The daughter of the late Fred Bylow of Toledo, Ohio, Lynn had been active with the atomic veterans for a number of years. Her father had died in 1982 at the age of fifty-four after fifteen years of illness due to radiation exposure. A navy veteran, Fred was a Pharmacist's Mate Third Class on the USS *Bottineau*. In 1946, the *Bottineau* was among the fleet of ships ordered to Bikini Atoll in the Pacific to observe the testing of two atomic bombs. From the age of fifteen, Lynn suffered from a whole range of illnesses including tumours, fevers, a hysterectomy and intestinal and kidney disease. During my five-week stay in the United States I would get to know Lynn well and realise what a tough lady she really was. One night as I chatted to her about all her medical problems she partially lifted up her blouse to show me the state her young body was in. My eyes filled up with tears as I gazed at her abdomen and chest which were ravaged with scar tissue.

It was all I could do to stop myself from completely breaking down in front of her.

Our hotel was located in New York itself and we soon settled down to the task of mapping out our touring schedule. During our stay we would visit almost sixteen cities throughout the length and breadth of the United States. All the journeys would be done via the internal shuttle flights which hop between the urban sprawls on an unbelievably regular basis. We soon made the acquaintance of other veterans who had travelled from all over the planet to take part in the tour. We met Cornelis Van Munster, a Dutchman by birth, who was brought up in Australia. Con worked near Ground Zero after the Maralinga blasts in Australia where he was stationed with the Australian Army Engineering Corps. After being exposed to levels of radiation which were far above the permissible levels, he was discharged from active service in 1958. He became the President of the Australian Veterans Association in 1979 and was visiting the US in this capacity when I met him in 1984. Another veteran who we soon got to know well was Al Draper, representative of the Canadian servicemen who had witnessed nuclear tests in Christmas Island, Australia and Nevada. Al had himself participated in the Nevada blast named "Plumbbob" which was detonated at the Nevada Test Site in June of 1958. Six months later he had suffered complete paralysis, a condition which still haunted him when we met in New York.

After a couple of nights in New York we headed for Boston, Massachusetts, where we were greeted by a proclamation from the city's mayor, Mr Raymond Flynn. This statement read:

> Between 1945 and 1963 more than 250,000 U.S. servicemen and women witnessed the 235 nuclear explosions conducted by the U.S. Government, or served in forces occupying Hiroshima and Nagasaki at the conclusion of World War II. During this same period, military personnel of Great Britain, Canada, Australia, France, New Zealand, and the Soviet Union, similarly witnessed nuclear weapons explosions.
>
> The formation of the International Alliance of Atomic Veterans is an historic occasion, one to which we should give proper recognition. It marks the coming together of patriotic veterans from around the world who are both witnesses and victims of nuclear testing.
>
> Atomic Veterans offer a compelling argument for an end to nuclear weapons testing. They have served their countries with honour and dignity. Their call for a Comprehensive Test Ban

Treaty as a first step toward ending the nuclear arms race is one that the world's governments cannot ignore.

Therefore, I, Raymond L. Flynn, Mayor of the City of Boston, do hereby declare Tuesday, May 15, 1984, to be International Atomic Veterans Day throughout the city of Boston, a day dedicated to those patriotic men and women the world over who bear solemn witness to the horrors of the nuclear arms race.

This day shall be a time for us to reaffirm the call for an end to nuclear weapons testing as a first step toward ending the dangerous continuation of the nuclear arms race.

With hardly a breath to spare we flew on to the next city where, like Boston, we would be guests at a massive cheese and wine reception. After the socialising we would all take turns lecturing to the invited audience before the main speaker, usually Anthony Guarisco, would invite questions from the audience. After two or three weeks of this activity I was ready to drop and I found myself using a walking-cane to help me get around.

One of the largest and most intimidating venues I attended was the University of Utah where we were faced by rows and rows of chairs which were filled by hundreds of bright, young students who were keen to ask us every conceivable question on our experiences. I wasn't used to this type of set-up and on more than one occasion I had to grope around my brain for decent answers. But, after it was all over, I felt as if I had really learned something: know your facts and know them well!

One of the cities that I'll never forget was, needless to say, Las Vegas. I thought that I might have liked this place but the moment I saw it in the flesh I realised what a dump it really was. Everyone seemed to be going nowhere fast and the noise drove me round the bend. I stayed in the main part of this city for a few hours before I gladly retreated back to join the rest of the entourage.

As we all ate dinner I couldn't help noticing that the chap next to me was shaking like a leaf. I started chatting to him and soon found out he was an American Test Veteran who had witnessed a number of large explosions in the nearby Nevada Test Site where, ironically, we were due to visit the following day. I didn't need to ask him why he was shaking since his face betrayed the fact that he was quite clearly terrified.

"You don't think there might still be radiation around here, do you Mr McGinley?" he probed.

I did my utmost to try and calm this man's fears but I knew my words were wasted since his panic was buried beyond the reach of even the most penetrating advice. As we drove out to the Nevada Test Site to hold a small rally, the man shook violently. His eyes stared straight ahead and his shirt was soaked in sweat. Some other Americans took him away and eventually calmed him down just long enough to hold our meeting. I felt really sorry for him and in a way I knew what he was going through. To the outside world he looked just like any fifty-year-old man but inside he was just an innocent twenty-year-old who was scared out of his skull.

A memorial service was held outside the Nevada Test Site. Everyone spoke at the service which was held under the shade of a large marquee which had been erected for the occasion. I strolled out into the blistering heat to look at the entrance. I thought I was alone but I turned round to see Anthony Guarisco standing behind me.

"Ken, let me ask you something," he joked.

"Sure, go ahead," I said.

"When was the last time you had a gun pointed at your head?" he said quietly.

I hesitated for a moment because I wasn't sure whether he was kidding or not.

"Look over my left shoulder," he said hardly moving his lips.

I looked over his shoulder. As I squinted my eyes against the desert sunshine, I could make out a small hill about four hundred yards down the road. On top of the hill was a gallery of rifles pointed at me by about five or six uniformed soldiers. I froze.

Suddenly a sheriff's car appeared on the scene. This broke the tension and I grinned as a Rod Steiger look-alike hauled himself out of the front seat. It was like a scene from a film and I was waiting on Sidney Poitier appearing at any moment.

"I hope you guys aren't going to cause any trouble here today!" he bawled.

"We're holding a memorial service and I'm not used to having guns pointed at me," I said.

"Uhuh, and where are you from?" he drawled.

"Great Britain and we don't do that sort of thing over there," I snapped as I motioned to the snipers.

The fat policeman looked around warily then he pulled his large belt up under his big gut.

"Yeh, well if there's any problems then you're to blame . . . mister," he sneered, before he waddled back over to his car.

Anthony put his hand on my shoulder and we stood watching the sheriff drive away. He didn't say anything to me because he didn't have to – I knew what he was up against.

I met another veteran who had taken part in a number of tests in the Nevada desert. He walked around on a crutch all the time because his spine was crumbling as a result of cancer. He told me that in those days his job involved taking the readings of the amount of radiation that the soldiers had been exposed to during the tests.

"After I'd taken the readings, which were usually way above the safety limit, I was required to mark them down into a large book," he said. "But I was told to keep *two* books. The first book contained the real, dangerously-high readings and that went straight to the AEC scientists. But the second book," he continued, "had charts which used fabricated figures, well below the safe dosage and that was what the press were fed with."

After he told me this I just shrugged my shoulders because I was starting to realise that nothing could really shock me anymore. I could also see the striking similarities between the American veterans and those of us from the UK. Apart from the more obvious overt parallels in our accounts about watching bomb test, I noticed the similarities in the eyes of the men. A BBC cameraman once told me that he found it really difficult to film atomic veterans because the film didn't pick up our eyes properly and the final shot also showed a strange redness on the skin of the person who was being interviewed. He said it was probably something to do with the radiation inside us since he checked and double-checked the quality of the film he was using. Although I didn't understand the cameraman's technical terminology, I could still identify with the point he was making. Anytime I met another atomic veteran I knew we had more in common that any onlooker might be able to see. It was the same story during the US trip and on more than one occasion I found myself chatting to men I'd never met before in a way that made us feel like long lost twin brothers. I knew deep-down that the very essence of our lives, our souls, had been marked forever by the same atomic stain.

Before we left the Nevada Test Site we unveiled a small monument to the world's atomic veterans. The inscription on the plaque simply read:

This monument is dedicated to the millions of people whose lives were sacrificed on the altar of the Atomic Age.

On the Memorial Day, May 28th, 1984, we the victims, together, call for an end to all nuclear testing.

So the children of the world may live in peace without these profane weapons.

It was early June when we arrived in Washington DC to give one of the last receptions on our itinerary. I had been looking forward to this occasion for some time since I knew I would be sharing the platform with Senator Edward Kennedy. I had long admired the late President Kennedy and his brother, the former Attorney General, Robert Kennedy. Indeed, a year after I was married, I wrote to President Kennedy and asked him to send me a signed photograph of himself so that I could hang it up in our new house. A month or so later I received a lovely photograph of the president and the first lady along with their two young children. It was signed to me by Mrs Kennedy. That photograph still stands in my house and I had a small Polaroid of myself and my wife holding it when I eventually met Senator Kennedy in Washington. I chatted to him for a moment or so then I showed him the little snap. He gazed at it for a moment or two in silence.

"Is that Jack?" he asked hesitantly.

"Yes," I answered. "I got that a year after he became President. I had just got married myself and things were looking good for the future. I suppose I was a bit naïve and innocent back then," I said.

"We all were," he said slowly. Then he took the small photograph off me and signed it. He'd made my day and apart from meeting Mrs Corretta King, the widow of Dr Martin Luther King, it was one of the most memorable parts of the whole trip.

The same afternoon we received editions of the Washington newspapers which underlined the effect our campaign was having on the American politicians:

WASHINGTON (AP) – Forty senators served notice they will press for legislation directing President Reagan to seek an immediate resumption of negotiations with the Soviet Union for a complete ban of nuclear weapons tests.

"We believe that a comprehensive test ban treaty is readily attainable and readily verifiable," Sen. Edward M. Kennedy, D-Mass, said Thursday. "It is an important first step toward a complete freeze on the nuclear arms race. It will halt the race toward even more dangerous, even more potent and ever more accurate nuclear warheads."

Republican Sen. Charles Mathias of Maryland agreed, saying, "If there is anything I would like to do with my life, I want to make sure that never again will anyone on this Earth experience the effects of a nuclear blast."

We arrived back in London a little bit lighter (I'd lost half-a-stone) and a great deal wiser. Some representatives from Greenpeace met us and we were taken back to our hotel which was in the middle of the city. On the return journey to Britain I was delighted to have the company of Anthony Guarisco who had decided to come back to the United Kingdom with me for a short holiday. The Greenpeace welcoming committee said that they had laid on a special coming-home present for us. We didn't have a clue what they were talking about but played along since they were footing most of the bills. We journeyed the short distance to the wharf where the Greenpeace boat was berthed and they told us what their plans were. When we heard what they were going to do we almost died. The next morning everyone else, including every single London newspaper, soon found out what they were up to as well . . . A member of Greenpeace had climbed Big Ben outside the Houses of Parliament and hung a gigantic sign from the top of it. The volunteer then sorted a hammock for himself and promptly fell asleep, until he was arrested the following day. The message on this massive sign read:

"TIME TO STOP NUCLEAR TESTING!!!"

About twelve months later I was awoken by a long-distance phone-call. The international operator said that the call was from a Ms Suzuki in Japan. I was half asleep when I took the call so I told the operator to put the young lady through – perhaps she's wanting bed and breakfast I thought to myself.

"Are you Mr McGinley?" asked the strange voice.

I told her that I was and she proceeded to introduce herself to me. She was indeed called Suzuki and she was a member of a peace organisation from Japan which was in the last stages of planning a massive memorial gathering in remembrance of the fortieth anniversary of the dropping of atomic bombs on Hiroshima and Nagasaki.

"We have heard of the British Nuclear Test Veterans Association," she said. "Would you please come and attend our gathering, on its behalf?"

After some long talks with Alice and a meeting of the BNTVA's executive committee I decided to take the chance and go to Japan. Again, like the trip to America, this was an all-expenses-paid excursion with all the bills being met by the Japanese authorities. I had a rudimentary knowledge of the bombings of Nagasaki and Hiroshima and I knew I would find people who were suffering illnesses which were similar to those which many of the BNTVA's members had developed.

As I mentioned earlier, the US Government tested their first nuclear device, "Trinity", on 16 July 1945, at 5.30a.m. Some five days later on 21 July, Winston Churchill was passed a handwritten note during a session of the Potsdam Conference. The note read "Babies satisfactorily born." This was a macabre reference to the results of the Trinity test. A few weeks later, on 6 August, Colonel Paul W. Tibbetts Jr, from Miami in Florida, boarded the plane, Enola Gay, named after his mother, a native of Iowa. The plane headed for the Japanese city of Hiroshima and at precisely 8.15a.m. and seventeen seconds, when the early morning rush-hour was at its height, the Enola Gay unloaded a uranium bomb. Approximately forty-three seconds later, the bomb, named "Little Boy", detonated, causing a fireball to burst open which was 18,000 feet across, with a temperature in its centre reaching some 100 million °F. The initial flash blinded thousands, and four square miles of the city immediately vanished. Anyone near the centre of the detonation simply evaporated. Others saw the skin slide down their arms and fall off on to the ground in front of them, exposing raw tissue and white bones. There was death everywhere in all its vulgar forms. Three days later an atomic bomb made of plutonium was dropped on the city of Nagasaki. The military establishment apparently wanted to see how this bomb, made of a different substance from the earlier Hiroshima bomb, would perform. The human suffering which resulted soon gave them their answer.

A young member of the Marine Transport relief team described his duties in the immediate aftermath of the bomb being dropped on Hiroshima:

> In corpses near ground zero the eyeballs were blown outside their heads. The skin was a black-tinged yellowish brown and very dry; it was clear that these persons had died in agony. Whether they were incinerated instantly by the intense heat, or were crushed

by the immense blast force, theirs was an instant death from a sudden flash and blast of proportions beyond imagination. It is not clear whether the dead found in burned-out streetcars had died first and then burned along with the streetcars, or had been burned to death by the flaming streetcars, but the bones were not bleached white. Many corpses were found at places where there was water – rivers, old wells, cisterns, ponds, and the like. Persons who did not die instantly had, it appears, exerted themselves to the limit in their search for water.

As the days passed, our main job became disposal of corpses. All of them were cremated; and as firewood was in short supply, we had to use fuel oil and gasoline. Ashes and bone remains of unidentifiable corpses were gathered in each local district and buried in temporary graves, on which were placed simple markers. Identifiable remains were sorted out to give to surviving families, but no one came to receive some of these remains.

On the fifth day we were assigned to disposal of the countless corpses floating in the river, bobbing up and down with the waves caused by the ebb and flow of the tide. The corpses were retrieved by boat and transported to shore. Several dozen bloated, naked bodies lined up was a sight too gruesome to look upon. When we reached out and grasped the hand of a decayed corpse, the skin just slipped off . . .

The horrific nature of this narrative is heightened still further when one remembers that this account just refers to the initial deaths which immediately followed the detonation of the atomic bombs. It was only later that people who hadn't been anywhere near the explosion, both in Hiroshima and Nagasaki, suddenly began to fall ill and die in a most horrendous way. The real horror came when the incidence of leukaemia, other cancers, genetic disorders and cataracts began to rise.

These terrible details rattled around inside my head as I flew to Japan to participate in the peace conference. Before I left I'd been sent a letter by Anthony Guarisco who had heard about my invitation through the International Alliance of Atomic Veterans. His letter read:

Dear Ken,

In the very near future if events unfold as outlined in our last telephone conversation, you will soon be in Japan representing the BNTVA and the nuclear veterans of the IAAV. I'm sure when you were involved in nuclear testing as a young British soldier that it never entered your mind that one day you would be representing over one million nuclear veterans world-wide.

As a nuclear veteran and a member of the IAAV, I want to thank you for taking time out of your busy schedule as the Chairman of the BNTVA and also your private life to represent each of us, and I wish you good luck and God speed.

Since the day that I had the good fortune to be introduced to you, you have always proved to be an honest and sincere person who was not afraid to truly give of himself for the cause of the nuclear veterans. It is because of this knowledge, I realise that you will hold up under the gruelling work that awaits you in Japan. There will be times when you will be very tired and will wish that you had more rest, or better yet, at least eight hours sleep. Many of the "overseas" delegates will tire and not attend some of the meetings that last into the early mornings. The Japanese will judge each delegate by their sincerity and their willingness to hang in there and participate in the many meetings and events. It's not easy and you will deserve a good rest when you return to your loved ones in Dunoon.

The Japanese know much about nuclear veterans and will want to know even more about them, especially about the British. It's a golden opportunity to let them know about the callous attitude of the British government towards the nuclear veterans . . . Good luck to you again my good friend. When you make your first speech at the first meeting in Tokyo or wherever, please convey my deepest respect and best wishes to all the Hibakusha, overseas delegates and all our Japanese brothers and sisters, for indeed we are . . . all God's children.

I arrived in Tokyo and jumped aboard a plane to Hiroshima. We spent a few days there and I visited the peace-park together with hundreds of thousands of veterans of the atomic-bomb attack forty years before. The people were really nice to me when they realised who I was and what I represented. The name Hiroshima conjures up images of devastation but nowadays this isn't the case. The city is lovely and bright although the epi-centre of the bomb site is still preserved to remind the population of that terrible day.

After a few days I caught a "bullet"-train to Nagasaki. That journey was truly amazing and I remember being surrounded by loads of young schoolchildren who all laughed at my strange Scottish accent. I passed around a gigantic bag of sweets to all these kids and they got so excited I eventually had to ask them to stand aside so that other passengers could pass by. It proves my theory that children really are the same the whole world over.

The Japanese people have a lovely custom which consists of giving anyone who they meet a small gift. I never failed to be touched by the way that I would be presented with something as small as a key-ring which had been carefully wrapped up and labelled for me.

When I finally got off the train in Nagasaki I was met with a barrage of questions from a whole pile of journalists and reporters who were waiting for all the guests to arrive. They asked me all sorts of questions about the association and wanted to know the reasons why I had decided to journey all the way to Japan to take part in this important occasion. Some messages had already arrived ahead of me, from people like Anthony Guarisco. Tony Benn MP also sent a touching message which read:

> Dear Friends in the Peace Movement,
> I am very sorry that I am not able to attend the Hiroshima/ Nagasaki Fortieth Year International Forum in Tokyo to commemorate the fortieth anniversary of the atomic bombing of the two Japanese cities. Having been in Tokyo two years ago I greatly wish I could be there this year to emphasize the international solidarity there is for those who are opposed to atomic weapons and favour detente, co-operation and peace. The current initiatives towards a Star Wars programme are a deadly threat to the survival of mankind and I know the Japanese peace movement in all its forms will want to join in preventing that from occurring.
>
> In peace, Tony Benn, MP

I visited a special hospital in Nagasaki, set aside for the exclusive treatment of patients affected by the atomic bombs. Old people who actually witnessed the explosions are treated alongside youngsters who suffer genetic disorders incurred as the result of exposure to radiation. I met one old lady who had been injured by the Nagasaki bomb in 1945. This proud woman had flinched and drawn away from me when I put my hand out to greet her. I didn't realise that her hand was badly deformed as a result of the post-detonation heat blast, but, even after I was told, I still put my hand out to her. Someone quickly told her who I was and what the BNVTA badge stood for. When she heard all about me she began to cry and opened her arms out to me. I cried myself when I gave her a big hug, and after I'd toured the hospital ward she presented me with a lovely bunch of Japanese flowers which she'd asked a nurse to give her.

I spoke in a university in Nagasaki before I left to come home. I remember asking for directions to the stage from a young organiser. He simply pointed to an innocent-looking corridor which had a small flight of stairs at the very end of it. I walked along the tunnel and mounted the stairs. When I reached the top step I almost fainted with shock . . . I was facing a crowd of tens of thousands of students who were seated in what resembled a football stadium! I meekly took my seat and waited my turn to be called to speak. When I was introduced, the chap at the podium said that I was from England. When I heard him say this I waved my arms wildly and said that I was from Scotland. I didn't realise everyone could hear this remark and I nearly died when the whole crowd started to laugh and cheer. I was annoyed with myself for, as far as I could see, getting off on the wrong foot and I began to shake when I started my speech. I can vaguely remember a little of what I said:

> When man discovered the secret of the atom he condemned countless thousands of his fellow men to death and lingering disease. The awesome power of the atom – the very building block of the universe – has been used for the purposes of war and destruction. The citizens of Hiroshima and Nagasaki have the terrible distinction of being the first victims of the atomic bomb. We have all been humbled by the terrible suffering which has been graphically shown to us during this forum . . .

In a sudden burst of inspiration I ended my statement with three short sentences which I roared out like a Glasgow union man during the UCS strike of the 1970s:

> 'No more Hiroshima! No more Nagasaki! No more Hibakusha!'

The last Japanese phrase actually means "survivors of the bomb" and when I said these simple words I really meant them. As I sat down I heard a terrible sound, like thunder rumbling. The last time I'd heard anything like it was when I had witnessed the earthquake with wee Frank in San Francisco all those years before. I looked up in panic to see where the sound was coming from. I couldn't believe my eyes when I saw the whole stadium rise to its feet to applaud my words. I sat in my chair and shook with nerves . . .

Before I left Japan for the journey home I met a woman that I'd wanted to speak to for years. Dr Rosalie Bertell is an American Roman Catholic nun who also happens to be one of the world's greatest

127

experts on the effects of radiation. When her book *No Immediate Danger* was published it was greeted with academic acclaim the world over and she was also one of the patrons of the BNTVA, so I was looking forward to speaking to her. When I did meet her I wasn't disappointed and I can safely say that she is one of the kindest and most intelligent people who I've ever met in my life. She even joined a few of us when we went out on the town for a few drinks one night and she surprised everyone by downing a very large pint of beer in preference to a more "nun-like" glass of white wine!

As I left to go home she presented me with a little poem that she'd written. I feel that her words identify a fear which many veterans of nuclear tests carry inside them:

Passioned Stillness

will the whole world be silent after the
                                    bomb drops?
will the birds chirp?
will the frogs call to one another in the wet
                                            grass?
will a baby cry?

and when the dust and ash and black rain
                                settle on the earth
will the water try to wash the stones?

what will they think – the tortured sterile
                        children of the black earth?
will they wonder how we did it with such
                                    noble motives
    – saving democracy
    – congratulating ourselves over a blast-off
                        which killed the grass
    – adoring the twisted steel and melted
                cables bought with the bread of the
                                            poor?

will the cherry blossoms ever be seen again?
will anyone ever sing?

or can we hear the passioned stillness now and
                                    turn away?

Rosalie Bertell

Chapter Six

ON MY RETURN to Dunoon after my sixteen-day trip to Japan I noticed that my wife, Alice, and daughter, Louise, had missed me badly. I felt rather guilty about this since I began to realise that I was devoting more time to the BNTVA than I was to my family and the guest house.

Most of the business in the guest house comprised families from the nearby American Navy base. Many of these servicemen were posted to Dunoon for two years or more, so they used guest houses as halfway houses before they moved into more permanent accommodation. I counted many of them among my best friends and to this day I still keep in touch with quite a number. Having been in the forces myself I could appreciate how lonely many of those young men become when they're so far away from home and I often turned a blind eye during some of their rowdier moments. The only thing I wouldn't put up with was drug-taking. On several occasions I came across "works", indicating that the military personnel were taking more than a few cans of lager to get high. My first reaction was usually to fling the culprits head-first out the door. But later, after I'd thought about it, I contacted the local police who were only too delighted to use whatever information I could supply them with since they were desperate to catch the bigger fish (usually Scottish I might add) who were actually pushing the stuff.

It was late 1985 when I noticed that business was starting to fall away to almost nothing. At first I thought that my anti-drug stance might have had something to do with this, but the police told me there was absolutely no way that this could be the case. A close American friend, however, took me to one side one afternoon and told me the real reason. He said that a few neighbours who had seen me on the television campaigning for the British Nuclear Test Veterans Association had started a rumour that I was a Communist! When I heard this I almost fainted with shock. I have never been a member of any political party in my life and if I was going to join any it certainly wouldn't be the Communist Party. I'm straight down the line Conservative or Labour, depending what mood I'm in.

After the initial shock of being told that everyone thought I was a Communist had sunk in I started to consider the implications this was going to have for me and my family. In the short-term it was blatantly clear that my name had been taken off the housing-list for US servicemen so business wasn't going to get any better. And those American guests that I still had staying were doing their damnedest to get out of our house as quickly as they could. In the longer term I knew that I could always publicly give up the BNTVA and stay where I was and hope that things improved. I thought long and hard before I decided to move house rather than give up my fight for the veterans.

Alice and I had tons of second thoughts before we finally moved back to Johnstone in 1986. Although our new house was lovely I felt as guilty as hell about taking the family away from Dunoon. The guest house on the sea-front was the perfect environment for any child to grow up in and I used to love taking Louise for long walks along the shore at night. To give all that up and leave it all behind was heartbreaking. Alice never ever said a word to me but I could tell that on a few occasions deep down she would rather I'd given up the association. But I'd gone too far to turn back. The BNTVA had become a part of my life and it had given me the opportunity to do things that I never thought were possible. Having to turn my back on one of the happiest chapters of my life was the price I was paying for daring to fight for men whose only crime was serving their country.

Within a few months of arriving back in Johnstone I noticed that my telephone was giving me lots of trouble. A British Telecom worker in Dunoon had told a friend of a friend that my number was being tapped. At first I laughed this off but the more I thought about it, and the more people I spoke to, I began to think that it might just be happening. By the time I moved into our new house in Johnstone I was beginning to get a bit paranoid, a condition which wasn't helped by the fact that the association received a letter which had clearly been opened. The package had a Ministry of Defence stamp on it and it had been resealed rather badly so it didn't take James Bond to work out who was on to us. When we made enquiries about the reasons for this intrusion into the association's business, the MOD spokesman said that the package might have contained drugs. The real reason, of course, was simply that the sender of the letter was the US Defence Nuclear Agency; they were sending us some basic background information which was freely available to any member of the public who cared to send them an internationally stamped-addressed envelope.

During this period the association acquired one of its most important recruits, a new secretary named Sheila Gray. Having worked with this woman for some time I can safely say that she is one of the toughest and most remarkable human beings that I have ever had the good fortune to know. I could tell you all about her but I won't, I'll let Sheila explain in her own words how she and her husband, Frank, became part of the BNTVA:

> Frank and I met on his return from the first atomic test – Oct 3 1952, Monte Bello. He was a happy carefree young man of 22 years, a mop of black wavy hair and we thought, a fit man. You had to be fit to be a marine!
>
> We married in July '53 and in Jan '54 we lost our first baby; I was only four months pregnant when I lost it. The "baby" was just a triangular piece of liver-like substance with a small round knob at one point, I presume the head.
>
> Two months later Frank was invalided out of the marines, his discharge papers said "Fundamental Dyspepsia of the Stomach". That was the beginning of his illnesses. His hair began to fall out, his teeth went bad and he had constant stomach pains.
>
> In Jan '56 we thought our luck had changed – we were blessed with a gorgeous baby boy, Michael. He was perfectly formed, bright and intelligent and a pleasure to have. We counted our blessings and looked forward to life again. How little we knew.
>
> In September '57 we had a daughter, Raine. She was born with a hole in her stomach and had to be propped up, day and night from birth, to allow her to take in food. When she was four she spent months in hospital with kidney problems, at six she contracted asthma – more time in hospital. Since she has grown up her hair has thinned dramatically, had a tumour removed from her neck, suffered Bell's palsy, had one miscarriage, two children born with eczema and one other who is hyper-active.
>
> In Feb '62 we had another son, Timothy. He was born premature and was nearly a month old before we knew he would live. He did, but at six years old was diagnosed as having duodenal ulcers. When he was twelve he began having severe migraine attacks and in his early twenties he was told his heart was weak. He has two sons, the youngest of which has no bridge to his nose, thus suffering nasal problems.
>
> Our last attempt at having children ended in June '67 when

I miscarried at six and a half months. When it was born it had no genitals! The nurse and I decided it was a boy because of the shape of its face. I was given no explanation, nothing.

After all this we still did not connect anything to the A-bomb. Frank had not been told of any danger attached to his participation, in fact all he had been told was he may be sterile for a few years but as he and the others were only young they thought that was great, they could have their fun and not have to worry. Even at this late stage we were using the bomb as "our claim to fame". Who else in our circle of friends could say they had witnessed such an event!

1972 arrived and Frank had a stroke. Luckily he recovered. Then the rot set in. He started with arthritis and his stomach pains returned with a vengeance. In 1974 he began getting mysterious swellings which were so painful he couldn't walk.

1978 saw his first angina attack and since then he has had many more. He has been told his bones are crumbling and will end his days in a wheelchair. Because of the state of his bones he cannot have more than one operation on his legs to relieve the pain.

The next part of him to deteriorate were his eyes. He had cataracts removed when he was in his twenties and now he has a rare condition called Françoise Dystrophy.

He underwent a blood test in New York in 1987 and it showed he had been irradiated. All this information has been presented to the MOD and they still maintain he was not harmed in any way and the test was perfectly safe! As it was the first test, and if they were so sure of their facts about safety, why hold the "test" in the first place.

I too have been a "victim" of the MOD's dogmatic approach to their servicemen and their families. In 1968 I went into an RAF hospital to have a trapped nerve in my right wrist released. They released it and trapped others! The following year I had to have another operation to release them, plus a similar operation on my left wrist. The surgeon cut the main nerve in my right wrist but told me "Not to worry but there had been a little mistake, he had cut the nerve by accident but don't worry, he had tucked it up my arm out of the way!" Over the next five years I had eight operations until finally I was told "Why do you keep bothering us, there's nothing more we can do – go away". This was when I decided I would sue. No such luck, I was informed; because my husband was in the services I could not sue and that was that. I was left at the age of forty, a cripple in both hands.

Still life goes on. I watched Frank slowly getting greyer and more ill. Then in June '83 someone told us the BBC were looking for men who had taken part in nuclear tests. Frank sent off his particulars and within a couple of weeks he received a letter from Ken to say he was holding a meeting in Newcastle and would he attend. That was the beginning of the busiest time of our lives. Frank undertook to start a branch of the association in his area and search for other veterans. He did this with some success but a year later had to step down because of his ill-health. Instead he took on the job of National Treasurer – a more sedentary position.

I began to accompany him to committee meetings because I too was interested . . . and what an eye-opener! After talking to other veterans and their wives, all our problems fell into place. We all seemed to be suffering similar problems. It couldn't just be coincidence. We all came from different walks of life, the men all had different jobs, we all lived in different parts of the country BUT they had all witnessed nuclear explosions! I now reflected on the two babies we had lost. Instead of being relieved they had not lived with horrible deformities I realised we should have had two healthy and lively children – all because of the "safe" nuclear tests. At one of the committee meetings the association was without a secretary. I offered to stand in for three months until a new one was found to take over the position. I am still doing the job! It has been an enlightening time and I have met some very brave men. I watch them growing more ill as each day passes and sadly many have died. I have met some distinguished people of whom I am ashamed and others I will always be proud to know. The people who will always stay in my thoughts, however, are our widows. Even in their grief they find the strength to carry on the fight for justice which their husbands began. Our various governments are a disgrace to our country when they refuse to acknowledge that mistakes were made, mainly through ignorance of radiation and its effects – or is it that the mistakes are too big to admit to!

Earlier, I stated our first child was a perfect boy and so he was. He was intelligent – four A-levels, ten O-levels; at nineteen he was qualified to be an electronics officer in the RAF but because he was overweight he was not accepted. He rose above this disappointment, met a girl and settled down and had two beautiful children. When they were three years and eighteen months old he went to work one day and never returned. He worked at ICI and was inspecting some pipes which held liquid ammonia, an unforeseen metal fatigue fractured a pipe and the liquid was forced out at a tremendous pressure. Our perfect child was no more.

This tragedy was the last straw for Frank and he had to finally admit he was too ill to work any more. So at the age of fifty-nine he is now a permanent invalid. Indeed at this moment he is back in hospital with another mysterious swelling. How much more is one man expected to take. If there is a God and I believe there is, we all need Him now. We are not asking for anything we are not entitled to, just a fair hearing and justice. The men served their country in the 1950s, now let the country serve them in their hour of need.

Sheila's words speak for themselves and as Vietnam veteran Ron Kovic once said when describing his own life, "they pour on to the page like a scream". The reason that I included her story is simply to underline the fact that the association is full of individuals like her who go through more suffering in one day than most people experience in the course of their entire lives. Both Sheila and Frank deserve better.

In the early hours of 26 April 1986, in the area of the Soviet Union known as the "breadbasket of Russia", a nuclear accident occurred at the Chernobyl complex. Initially, the rest of the European mainland received only the barest details relating to this incident. By 28 April Scandinavian scientists began to take readings on their equipment which suggested that the recent rain had contained dangerously high levels of radiation. Meteorological enquiries pointed to the Soviet Union as being the most likely source of this cloud. Some twelve hours later a brief statement was issued by the USSR Council of Ministers:

> An Accident has taken place at the Chernobyl power station, and one of the reactors was damaged. Measures are being taken to eliminate the consequences of the accident. Those affected by it are being given assistance. A government commission has been set up.

Even a layman like myself could read between the lines of this statement and see that the accident was much, much worse than official sources would admit. The scale of the clean-up operation was enough to convince even the sceptics of the serious nature of this incident. For some ten days the Soviet services fought a round-the-clock battle in an attempt to dampen the fire and contain the radioactivity. Over thirty lives were lost during this hazardous operation and many more were wrecked due to exposure to high levels of radiation. The radioactive cloud had contaminated farms and livestock throughout Europe and Scandinavia, thereby entering the food-chain system. Western European governments responded to the widespread public concern in varying degrees ranging from panic to complacency. By 1987, one expert had forecast that the worldwide death-toll as a result of the Chernobyl accident would reach the 40,000 mark. Some 12,000 of that figure would belong to the population of the Soviet Union. I'm sad to say that subsequent press reports began to confirm my worst fears. In 1988 *The Lancet*, for example, published research which suggested that a thirty-seven per cent increase in the incidence of leukaemia in Scotland might be linked in some way to the Chernobyl accident.

When news of the accident at Chernobyl first hit the world's headlines I was as shocked as anyone else. But I knew that the story would fade away and be replaced with something else much quicker than the real effects of the radiation would. I contacted the Russian Embassy in London and offered my support to the brave Russian firemen who had put out the blaze which had raged during the dangerous ten-day operation. I knew that these men had risked life and limb to save lives, not only in their own country but also throughout the whole of Europe, and I felt that the nuclear test veterans who I represented had something in common with them. I also told the Russian official that I hoped the authorities would treat these "nuclear veterans" much better than our government had treated us. I think he was slightly taken aback by this direct approach but he thanked me profusely and said that the would pass on my best wishes to the Kiev firemen. As I replaced the handset of the telephone I wondered if I had done the right thing or not since everyone else had been criticising the Soviet Union for not releasing enough information about the disaster when it first happened. Whilst I agreed with this I couldn't help feeling sorry for the men who were in the front line, doing their utmost to clean up the mess that others had made. I knew that their future would be, at best, uncertain, and at worst, beyond their most terrible nightmares.

A few weeks later, in June 1986, I was contacted by Intourist, the official Russian travel agency, who offered to pay for me to travel to the Soviet Union to meet some of the firemen who I had expressed concern about. This invitation came completely out of the blue and when I contacted other members of the association they all urged me to go ahead and make the trip. The tour would take in Moscow, Kiev and Leningrad and I would be accompanied by Alan Rimmer and Randolph Caughy from the *Sunday People* newspaper and Brian Hitchins, the editor of the *Daily Star*. Some local fire stations gave me a plaque to present to the Russian firemen and I was also given a plaque by Renfrew District Council, to present to the City of Kiev. Strathclyde Regional Council, which represents nearly half the total population of Scotland, gave me a message of goodwill for the fire-fighters and workers at Chernobyl. It read as follows:

> On behalf of the people of Scotland – almost half the population of Scotland – I send our grateful thanks to the brave men who lost their lives and others who risked theirs to prevent the disaster at Chernobyl from becoming an even bigger international nightmare.
>
> Without their selfless action the number of immediate victims would have been counted in thousands with many more thousands throughout Europe showing the effects of radiation over a long period of years.
>
> Strathclyde Regional Council has declared the region a nuclear-free zone, with the ultimate aim of ridding it of all nuclear installations. Accidents like those at Chernobyl make us more determined to carry this policy through to its logical conclusion.
>
> The people of Strathclyde thank the firemen and safety workers at Chernobyl and applaud their heroism.

Strathclyde Regional Council also gave me two footballs from two of the most famous clubs in the world, Celtic and Rangers, to present to Mr Leonid Teljatnikov, for his two teenage sons. Leonid was a thirty-five-year-old fireman from Kiev who had shown outstanding heroism when he'd jumped into pools of radioactive water during the clean-up operation. The balls were to be presented to his sons along with a box of chocolate tea-cakes from the well-known local confectioners, Tunnocks. (Leonid was far to ill to meet me during this trip but I sent the footballs and cakes on to him when I arrived in Kiev. Years later, in 1989, I attended another peace conference in Japan and who should I meet when I arrived there but Leonid! I walked up to him and said "Celtic and Rangers". He looked at me for a moment, grinned then replied in faltering English, "Tunnocks tea-cakes!" It's a moment I'll never forget for the rest of my life.)

During the flight to Moscow I sat beside Brian Hitchins, whilst

Alan sat beside Randolph. To pass the time Alan and Randolph played the schoolboy game of "battleships". This involves drawing a grid on a piece of paper then plotting out your "battleships" and "submarines" on to the various lines. Your opponent does the same, then you both shout out coded directions in an attempt to sink the other's forces. It was harmless fun until we all arrived in Moscow and the customs men happened to see all these military-looking drawings in Alan's notebook. Brian and I fell about the place laughing as a worried-looking Alan and Randolph tried to explain that they weren't from MI5!

Our first day in Moscow was very well organised with a chauffeur-driven car taking us on a sight-seeing tour of the city and later on a visit to the Kremlin. The hotel in which we stayed was the Cosmos which is the largest hotel in Europe, with accommodation for 7,000 people. The service was first-class, the food outstanding and the hotel was filled with tourists from places as far apart as Leeds and Las Vegas.

On 16 June we had a meeting with the Novasti Press Agency. It was more of a "Press to Press" conference dealing with the evacuation of residents living near to the Chernobyl accident. This was followed by a visit to the famous Bolshoi Ballet. When I went to the theatre to see the ballet I was half-asleep and wasn't exactly looking forward to the evening. But when the performance actually began my jaw dropped open at the sheer spectacle of the whole thing. I perked up, the two or three hours flew by and I can safely say it was one of the most entertaining nights I've ever had in my life. (Even as I write this I've to pinch myself: Ken McGinley from Johnstone enjoyed the Bolshoi Ballet in Moscow . . . wee Frank will never let me live this admission down – I can just hear him saying "Ballet? Nothing but skinny lassies and poofs in tights!")

A meeting of the USSR Peace Committee was held on 17 June and many questions were asked about the BNTVA and my own experiences of radiation. The first question thrown at us was: "What are you doing here?" As you can imagine we were quite taken aback but once we were allowed to speak, the atmosphere cleared considerably. My reply took the form "That the accident at Chernobyl and the obvious concern all over Europe, including my own country, at the high levels of radiation, were relevant to the claims of servicemen and civilians who participated in the British Nuclear Tests programme between 1952 and '62." I then went on to say that I was on a sincere goodwill visit from my country to present plaques to the brave firemen of Kiev who knew the dangers of radioactive contamination yet went ahead with their dangerous mission. I also stated that I was positive that all the members of our association had been brought up to respect tragedy and that sympathy was uppermost in their minds – not criticism and propaganda reports – and that this statement was sincere and not of a political nature.

I was made much more aware of the extent of the tragedy of Chernobyl when our party drove to the city of Kiev which is about eighty miles from the nuclear plant. The city was devoid of any young people and I never once saw a young mother walking along the street pushing a pram with a child in it. It was a rather eerie experience. However, we did manage to meet the First Deputy Chairman of Kiev City Council, Mr Nicholas Lavruchin, and the firemen, who I handed over the footballs to.

I attended a meeting of a peace committee in Moscow before I left the country. At one point during the meeting, rather a large dour-looking gentleman banged the table à la Khrushchev and said: "Dr McGinley, if the USA had released their studies on the effects of the radiation in Hiroshima and Nagasaki then we would be in a much better position to tackle the forthcoming problems at Chernobyl."

I winced when he called me "Dr" but I answered his politically loaded question as best I could: "Well, the Soviet authorities are right to criticise the American secrecy over Hiroshima and Nagasaki because I believe they were just experimental bombs which weren't really needed to end the war," I said. "But the Soviet authorities were, I feel, very slow to release their own information regarding the Chernobyl disaster. They were also extremely reluctant to admit that some of their own troops were, like the men I represent, deliberately exposed to radioactive fall-out after an atomic detonation in the South Urals in 1954. This horrific test was carried out by the Soviet Defence Authorities simply to establish what the effects of radiation on their armed forces were likely to be. But, in saying that, I must admit that it did take the government of my own country, the United Kingdom, almost thirty years to fill in important details surrounding the Windscale incident, so perhaps no one is perfect. The important issue now is how are you going to deal with all the victims of radiation, both in the short- and long-term?"

I received a rather vague and evasive answer to this question so I decided not to push the matter any further, but I couldn't help feeling that political pride was more important than people. This suspicion was confirmed in later years when the British Press printed articles relating to the way in which the Soviet authorities were treating their "nuclear veterans"; as recently as April 1990 a leading Sunday newspaper ran an article entitled "The Awful Truth About Chernobyl". The paper's correspondent in the city of Kiev wrote:

> Petya propped himself up in his hospital bed and despite the pain, struggled to put on a smile. His father was visiting the 12-year-old boy last week – one of the 130 child patients at a new clinic near Kiev, just 80 miles from Chernobyl. Both of them knew that Petya had only days to live as leukaemia relentlessly pursued its deadly course. It was difficult for the lad to talk but he wanted his father to have pleasant memories of him. He carelessly ran his fingers through his hair . . . dislodging a clump of shiny black strands. His father barely contained his tears. Another young victim of the Chernobyl nuclear disaster, the full horror of which is only now being revealed . . . Svitlana Kipyachenko is one of the founder members of the Mothers of Chernobyl group which is pressurising the Soviet Government to devote more resources to the victims of the tragedy and is organising an international conference about the disaster later on this month. She said: "After the catastrophe doctors treating victims had to sign statements swearing them to secrecy and they were ordered to attribute death to non-radiological causes . . . Hundreds of children are developing leukaemia and other carcinomas. Thousands show signs their immuno systems are breaking down. Babies are being born with severe defects and there has been a great increase in deaths at birth."

In my years as Chairman of the BNTVA I had received lots of letters which sketched out personal stories which reminded me of this tragic Russian story. Sadly, it served only to prove that my theory about the long-term effects of Chernobyl was correct. I'd rather have been proved wrong, of course.

Only a few weeks after I returned home from the Soviet Union I received a call from Mrs June Robinson, who was married to Alan "Tiny" Robinson. When I answered the telephone she simply said: "Alan's dead . . . ."

The last time that I'd met Tiny was when both him and June had paid me a visit in late 1985 when I was still staying in Dunoon. It was a wet Saturday afternoon when they rang the front doorbell of Pitcairlie. When I heard the door I automatically presumed that it was some tourists looking for a place to stay during the weekend when the local Highland Games were held. I couldn't believe my eyes when I opened the door to Tiny and his beautiful wife standing in front of me. It took me a minute or two to recognise Tiny because his face was a little thinner and his hair had turned grey, but once I realised who he was I immediately invited both him and June into the house. The last time that we'd seen one another had been nearly thirty years before on that cold winter's night when he'd waved wee Frank and myself off on the bus after we'd all returned from Christmas Island. We sat for a few hours and chatted about how life had treated us during the intervening years. I asked Tiny if he'd seen me in the news recently when I was campaigning on on behalf of the BNTVA. He didn't answer me directly so I didn't pursue that line of conversation any further. Only after his death did June tell me that Tiny hadn't been keeping too well and that he knew the bomb tests had something to do with it so obviously he didn't want to talk too much about the association or all its members who had also fallen into ill-health. With the benefit of hindsight I can fully understand this defensive reaction.

Alan "Tiny" Robinson went through hell during his last months alive. He was a mountain of a man, a man who loved his family and a man who could be relied upon. He worked like hell to provide his wife and son with the good things in life and he himself found pleasure in nothing more daring than a simple game of golf at the weekend. June told me that she had always wanted a large family when they had first got married. But Tiny revealed to her that he had heard stories of soldiers who had been on Christmas Island during the bomb tests being taunted by other soldiers: "They said that married men would father children who would be born looking like crocodiles," he'd told her. After years of pestering him, June finally persuaded Tiny to try for a child and they were both delighted when she finally gave birth to a lovely baby boy.

"When our son, Stewart, was born," recalled June, "Alan decided to quit while we were ahead. I think he thought we were lucky to have a perfectly healthy baby boy so he refused from that day on to ever have another child. There was something at the back of his mind worrying him. I knew it was those damn bomb tests."

June also told me that Tiny suffered from terrible skin-rashes, which flared up every seven years, and also from a series of ear complaints for which the doctors could find no real reason. These illnesses interfered with his work as a marine engineer, and he slowly began to complain more frequently about a pain which he had in his lower back. Over the next few months, he went through test after test and eventually entered hospital for an operation to remove a malignant tumour from his bowel. He recovered from this but the eventual decline in his health soon set in. The months which followed were the worst that June Robinson and her son will ever experience. She had to attend to Tiny twenty-four hours a day, making sure that his morphine was properly administered in order to relieve his pain whenever possible. June also remembers the remarks which Tiny made to her when they sat alone:

"He used to say things to me like, 'you'll never know what I've seen', or 'you'll never know what I'm thinking, June'. I knew in my heart that he was referring to the bomb tests. My Alan knew that those nuclear trials were the reason why he was dying but he was too proud and too patriotic to admit to it. My husband died for his country."

Tiny finally found peace at five to four on the morning of 24 June 1986. His death certificate states the cause of death as cancer of the colon but June discovered his poor body was riddled with more than one tumour. "He even had one in his brain," remarked June, "He was a beautiful man, a loving husband and a devoted father. I'll never rest until I get justice for all the other men who died in the same way as Alan did."

When June told me over the telephone that Alan "Tiny" Robinson had died I just started crying. We were so close yet so far away. In my mind's eye I will always see him as a gentle giant carrying a huge kit-bag as he entered our berth on the TT *Dunera* or as a thundering football player with legs like tree-trunks, ready to demolish any defenders foolish enough to go near him. By rights he should have lived out his life and grown old enough to be a grandfather but, like so many men who witnessed the bomb tests, this was not to be. If there is a heaven, and I believe there is, then big Tiny is there. He's right beside the veterans every step of the way in our fight for justice. The man is dead but his spirit lives on in us all.

Within the first few days of the BNTVA being born I was told that even if we could prove that a link existed between participation in the nuclear tests and subsequent illnesses, we would still find it well nigh impossible to obtain financial compensation from the British government. As early as 25 July 1983 David Alton had addressed this issue in the House of Commons:

. . . even if disease or death can be proved to have resulted from atomic test participation, there is still no guarantee of compensation under British law for servicemen or their relatives. Section 10 of the Crown Proceedings Act 1947 bars common law claims against the Crown by servicemen who sustain injury or disease that is attributable to their services.

And Labour's Frank Cook brought the BNTVA's arguments to the fore when he spoke about the same Act during a debate on 19 December 1984, when he said:

Britain has legislation – the Crown Proceedings Act 1947 – which precludes a member of the armed forces from taking legislative action to seek reparation for negligence during his period of service to the Crown. That legislation was dreamed up at a time when we had no knowledge of such operations, and no idea that they might occur in future. In this discussion we are considering a legacy of something about which we could not have known. Will the Government consider amending the Crown Proceedings Act to take account of the almost anachronistic failure of the legislation to cater for the future not only of those who have given good service to the Crown but of their offspring and future generations? We are talking about the suffering, of which we were unaware 30 years ago, of youngsters who may not be allowed to have children and who may have deformities that are even worse than those of their parents or grandparents. We are talking about things about which a legislative body has never before been forced to consider.

Section 10 of the Crown Proceedings Act was indeed the major obstacle. It was also a contemporary problem since lots of cases existed which did not involve nuclear-test veterans but which still brought into question the validity of keeping this piece of legislation on the statute book. Many young soldiers had been injured or killed in circumstances which should have led to the bereaved family being able to sue the negligent employer. But Section 10 of the Crown Proceedings Act ensured that no servicemen could ever sue the employer – technically, the Crown. A pressure group called Section Ten Abolition Group (STAG) was already in existence so the BNTVA also decided, at a meeting in Blackpool in late 1985, to take up the cudgels and fight this grossly unfair law. We knew we would have a hell of a fight on our hands since the government had fought off lots of other pressure groups in the past and, going on answers they were still giving in the House of Commons, they weren't suddenly going to change their minds. On 12 March 1984, for example, the Minister of State for Defence Procurement, Mr Geoffrey Pattie, commented:

> As to the rights of servicemen generally to claim compensation, the Crown Proceedings Act 1947 introduced the principle that the Crown would be in the same position as any private person in litigation. However, Parliament recognised when the Act was passed that it would not be acceptable for a serviceman, or the dependents of a deceased serviceman, to be able to bring an action for damages against the Crown and/or an individual serviceman on the grounds that the injury or death had been caused through the negligence of another member of the armed forces.
>
> Servicemen are called upon to risk injury and sometimes death not only in operations, but in training, and it would make the conduct of the armed forces impossible if a serviceman could bring an action against another serviceman, possibly his superior or subordinate in rank, or against the Crown, for alleged negligence during service activities. Therefore, provided that certain conditions are met, Section 10 of the Act bars any legal action against the Crown or a serviceman arising out of the death of or injury to another serviceman.

Whilst the government began drawing out the battle-lines for the war over Section 10, the BNTVA and STAG had managed to harness cross-party support from the House of Commons. Since the tragic death of Patricia Phoenix, the BNTVA had adopted the Labour MP and well-known campaigner for the disabled, Jack Ashley, as our patron. Jack was well respected on all sides of the House for his campaigning work and we knew his support carried considerable clout. Winston Churchill and Virginia Bottomley from the Conservative back-benches also supported our case, as well as others from across the floor like Gavin Strang and our old friend David Alton. The blatant injustices of Section 10 were tackled by Jack Ashley during a Commons debate on the issue, on 1 July 1986:

> The arguments by the Ministry of Defence for preserving Section 10 are ludicrous. It says, first, that there is no reasonable dividing

line between military action and other duties; secondly, that to abolish Section 10 would endanger discipline; thirdly, that its abolition would create anomalies; and fourthly, that servicemen may not be able to prove negligence. The first point is nonsense – any serviceman could tell the difference. Secondly, discipline has nothing to do with legal redress. Thirdly, the Ministry blithely disregards the anomalies that exist when a serviceman cannot sue, whereas other public servants can. Fourthly, whether a serviceman can prove his case is a matter for a court of law to decide, as happens with other public servants.

The association mapped out a strategy which we hoped would put so much pressure on the government that they would have no choice but to repeal Section 10. Up and down the country, we organised large rallies and collected tens of thousands of signatures on petitions. I got six nuclear-test veterans' widows, including June Robinson and Agnes Rettie, to travel down to London dressed in black. Those six brave women journeyed through to Whitehall to meet a minister from the Ministry of Defence, Roger Freeman, in order to present him with one of our huge petitions. When they actually arrived at the Whitehall building, they were met by an office minion who said that Freeman was too busy to come down in person. The six widows refused to move and eventually managed to corner Freeman as he was leaving the building via a less public exit. By this time the crowd was swollen with waiting press and TV crews who filmed and snapped away as Freeman squirmed with a mixture of shock, embarrassment and, above all, guilt.

On another memorable occasion, I spoke at a large STAG and BNTVA rally in Woolwich. I was accompanied by various ex-servicemen, who should have been allowed to sue the government, and also MPs like the ubiquitous Jack Ashley. As I delivered my speech on behalf of the nuclear-test veterans, potentially the largest group who would benefit from the repeal of the Act, a gigantic billboard was unfurled behind me. The billboard showed a soldier in a wheelchair and contained information about the unfairness of Section 10 of the Crown Proceedings Act. It was headed "WHAT THEY DON'T TELL THE PROFESSIONALS".

The various implications regarding the repeal of Section 10 were brought to the nation's attention when Winston Churchill put together a Private Member's Bill. The importance of this step, and the personal contribution made by Winston Churchill, cannot be overemphasised. He was fortunate in the respect that he managed to have his Private Member's Bill placed high up on the "running order" when the debate commenced. The Second Reading took place on 13 February 1987:

> Mr *Winston Churchill:* Of all the duties that Parliament has taken upon itself, few are more ancient in origin or more fundamental to the purpose of our being in this place than the redress of grievances. Predating by far the power to make or break Governments, redressing the grievances of the ordinary citizen against the overmighty power of the Crown or the Government has been seen by parliamentarians down the centuries to be one of the highest duties of our two Houses of Parliament . . . The Bill seeks to rectify an injustice that has become increasingly more glaring – discrimination that exists between members of the armed forces and the ordinary citizen in seeking damages in cases of injury or death arising from the negligence of others. An ordinary citizen or his dependents may sue through the courts and obtain substantial damages, but members of the armed forces are denied that right. This discrimination has given rise to much bitterness and a sense of injustice among those who have served their country loyally and suffered for it, not once, but twice – first, in suffering injury or death in the course of their duty and, secondly, in being denied the proper level of compensation that would be their due if they were in any other walk of life. I count myself fortunate that the opportunity has fallen to me to rectify this injustice . . .
>
> Mr *Jack Ashley:* This is a historic day for the armed forces. We are beginning the process of sweeping away legislation which has deprived servicemen and women of rights that have been enjoyed by everyone else, including all other public servants, such as police and firemen. I welcome the Bill warmly because it will remove an injustice, and I warmly congratulate the Hon. Member for Davyhulme [Mr Churchill] on his luck in the ballot, his choice of subject and his splendid speech . . . . The House should be ashamed that it allowed Section 10 of the Crown Proceedings Act 1947 to remain on the statute book for 40 years. I echo what J.S.C. Reid, later Lord Reid, said when he denounced the thinking behind the clause, as it then was, when the Bill was before the House in 1947. He condemned it as "A piece of departmental obscurantism and nothing else" . . . . Service men and women risk their lives in time of war – that is an acceptable doctrine – but they are entitled to defence against negligence in peacetime. The largest group of protestors against Section 10 are the nuclear-test veterans. About 20,000

took part in the atomic tests in Australia and the South Pacific in the 1950s and 1960s. In those days, the defence authorities' attitude to protection seemed as casual as if they had been at a Guy Fawkes bonfire party. But was that really so? I do not think that it was. A document marked "Top Secret" and dated 20 May 1953 from the defence research Policy Committee to the Chiefs of Staff states:

"The Army must discover the detailed effects of various types of explosion on equipment, stores and men with and without protection."

That means the soldiers must – it is not my word, but the word used in that secret document, *must* – be guinea pigs in discovering the effects of the explosions, without protection. Some of those men suffered grotesque and horrible deaths – there is no doubt or dispute about that – and others are still suffering severely. Anyone enduring such ordeals and written about in that way by military officials should at least have the right to some special consideration. The ugly thread of negligence runs through all those horror stories about the atomic tests as well as through the cases mentioned by the Hon. Member for Davyhulme and those I have described . . .

Mr Churchill: . . . The right Hon. Member for Stoke-on-Trent, South, spoke about the nuclear victims. It is an appalling fact that 20,000 British servicemen were involved in the British nuclear tests in Australia and the Pacific in the 1950s and 1960s, and undoubtedly large numbers were exposed to radiation. Indeed the right Hon. gentleman quoted part of a classified Ministry of Defence document of 1953 that appears to suggest that some servicemen were deliberately to be used as human guinea pigs to establish the effects of radiation on human beings. If that is true it was a most terrible thing for any British Government to have done. It defies belief especially when those tests took place so many years after the Hiroshima and Nagasaki bombs had been dropped with horrendous consequences for those populations. We have all seen the newsreel footage of some of those tests and have seen servicemen standing above ground with no protective clothing. They were ordered to turn away from the flash. At that blinding flash there was a massive discharge of gamma radiation and this was followed by the mushroom cloud billowing up. Successive Governments have refused to acknowledge that anyone involved in those tests suffered adverse health or premature death as a result of that exposure. However, the Government have slipped

146

up and that is made clear in the excellent brief provided by Dr Poole of the Library regarding the case of ex-Royal Marine George Pollard who died in 1978. That brief states:

> "The operation of Section 10 is typical of the labyrinthine complexity of Whitehall's bureaucracy, which effectively prevents compensation. Today if a serviceman, or his widow, declares an intention to sue the Government for damages, a "Certificate of Attributability" is issued automatically by the Ministry responsible for claims, the Department of Health and Social Security, under Section 10. This certificate admits that the condition suffered could be considered due to service but blocks any action in the Courts. The irony of the position is shown by the certificate issued in 1980 to a widow of an ex-serviceman who worked on a nuclear test site which, in order to avoid an action for damages, declares that the serviceman's death resulted from service on Christmas Island. Yet the Government's Official policy is to deny that any of the servicemen suffered because of those tests."

Winston Churchill's Private Member's Bill was duly passed on to the Committee stage via Standing Committee C on Wednesday 18 March. It was during this process that the possibility of making any compensation payments retrospective (i.e. back-dated to the time when the first Act was passed in 1947) was raised by Jack Ashley. Jack argued that there had been historical precedents of Parliament passing legislation which could be retrospectively applied, but the motion for this amendment was defeated by eight votes to six. This was something of a blow to the BNTVA but we sought consolation in the fact that the Bill seemed destined for a rapid third and final reading in the House of Commons.

On 24 April 1987, Mr Churchill's "Crown Proceedings (Armed Forces) Bill" received its Third Reading. In his opening remarks he said:

> I cannot fail to refer to the largest category of those who have received no compensation – the victims of British Nuclear Test programme. The Minister assured us in Committee that the report of the National Radiological Protection Board (NRPB), which was due by the end of last year, will definitely be available before the end of this year. In the event that the report shows, as many of us are convinced it will show, that among the 20,000 British servicemen who took part in those test programmes there is a significantly higher than average incidence

of cancer, leukaemia and other radiologically induced diseases, I find it inconceivable that the Government would not wish to move swiftly to provide full and fair compensation for those whose health had been destroyed in the course of their service to their country.

Jack Ashley commented:

. . . Quite honestly, we would not have this Bill without the efforts of Mrs. Carol Mills of the Section Ten Abolition Group (STAG) . . . [and] Ken McGinley and Sheila Grey of the British Nuclear Test Veterans Association . . .

The Third Reading continued, with more and more MPs jumping to their feet to congratulate Winston Churchill for all the hard work he'd put into preparing the ground for his Private Member's Bill, and for all the work that had been done by STAG, the BNTVA and others. It was clear that the Bill was going to pass its Third Reading with flying colours and that we were going to notch up a really historic victory.

During the debate several MPs alluded to the forthcoming results of the NRPB study as if they were a foregone conclusion. I couldn't help feeling that we were counting our chickens before they were hatched and, amid all the celebrations over the repeal of Section 10 on 24 April 1987, I began to have all those old doubts again about the impartiality of the NRPB. Until the report actually came out, however, I didn't have much information or evidence to back up these negative feelings. In the three years since the study had started I had become increasingly depressed as it became clear that the NRPB study was only examining the nuclear veterans who had already died. This was never the type of project that we'd envisaged. My good friend and a founder member of the BNTVA, Phil Munn, had been diagnosed as having leukaemia in 1982, yet he was still alive in 1987. The NRPB wouldn't be taking him into account, something which I thought was grossly unfair. In other words, the study was shaping up to be nothing more than a game of numbers. All the men who had fallen into ill-health with radiation-induced conditions which would eventually lead to a slow, pain-wracked, lingering and humiliating death were forgotten, simply because they were still alive.

All these worries, questions and doubts ran riot through my mind as we celebrated the success of the Section 10 campaign. The Third Reading of Mr Churchill's Bill had produced words of praise for his hard work, and optimistic advice for the BNTVA's next move. I had heard all these statements with pride but the one that really stuck in my mind was a much more cautionary remark made by Labour's Kevin McNamara:

> With regard to nuclear veterans, we have had an undertaking that the results of the survey will be announced by the end of the year. However, it is, after all, only a statistical survey. Some of us are still at a loss to understand why there must be a statistical survey, as that will take a long time to monitor and to reach conclusions about. We are not considering individual sufferers or complaints; we are merely considering a statistical exercise.

In short, the dumping of Section 10 had handed the British Nuclear Test Veterans Association a cocked pistol; only the right result from the NRPB study could provide the valuable ammunition.

Chapter Seven

AFTER MORE THAN four years of research, the NRPB eventually announced that it would publish its report looking into the "Mortality and cancer incidence in UK participants in UK nuclear weapon tests and experimental programmes".

The NRPB study had estimated that 22,347 servicemen took part in the twenty-one nuclear tests which were carried out by the United Kingdom between 1958 and 1962 in the South Pacific and Australia. Men who participated in subsequent clean-up operations were also included. The incidence of mortality in this group was compared with another "control" group of 22,326 servicemen who had served in tropical conditions during the same period.

Many of the members of the BNTVA were absolutely certain that such an apparently comprehensive study would show a direct link between participation in the bomb tests and subsequent ill-health. Privately, for all the reasons I've outlined earlier, I did not share this optimism.

The report was published in January 1988 and I was invited down to the press conference in London which was organised to publicise its findings. By that time I knew what conclusions had been reached by the NRPB since I had read about it in a "leaked" article which appeared in a quality newspaper that very morning. In the run-up to the publication of the report, the BNTVA had written to the NRPB to ask them for a confidential preview of their findings, so that we would be ready for the barrage of questions which was bound to follow. They refused this reasonable request point-blank and said that we would have to wait for the press conference. Consequently, you can imagine how I felt when I read that article in the newspaper as I waited for the press conference to start.

The report itself is exactly 124 pages long. It looks like a university undergraduate thesis and it is full of complex tables and graphs. Much of this numerical data is provided to help any keen statisticians who might happen upon the report whilst browsing through the library. If, like me, you are not scientifically-minded then you will probably find yourself jumping straight to the conclusions which are written near the end of the report. In plain English they tell you:

> It is concluded from this study that participation in the nuclear weapons test programme had not had a detectable effect on the participants' expectation of life nor on their total risk of developing cancer, apart from a possible effect on the risks of developing multiple myeloma and leukaemia . . .

After I read this short paragraph and then re-checked the much more detailed comments in the newspaper article, I felt my heart sink a little. Although I'd always known that it was highly unlikely that the NRPB were going to find in our favour, I'd always kept hoping that I would be proved wrong. But, after reading the conclusions, it appeared that my worst fears had been confirmed. The article in the newspaper certainly left no one in doubt about the report's contents and its banner headlines ran:

"ATOM TEST STUDY DENIES LINK TO SOLDIERS' CANCER"

I sat through the press conference feeling really depressed and I spoke to as many of the waiting reporters as I could before I left the building to head for the airport.

Over the next few weeks I took some time out to try and read through the report as best as I could. I openly admit that this was heavy and, at times, frustrating going. I made some notes in the margins against the areas that I thought were important, vague, evasive or surprising. Some other members of the BNTVA (especially the brilliant Mike Doyle) soon surfaced with their comments about the findings once they'd taken the time to digest it. When we collated our criticisms, we realised that the report wasn't as watertight as it had first appeared and that many of its basic mistakes were easily found if the reader didn't mind digging through all the mathematical formulae. Any points we made would be easy to hit over the head with an academic club, but we decided to go ahead anyway and publicly draw attention to the flaws which we had found.

Apart from my basic criticism that the NRPB should never have done the study in the first place, my main objection to the study was simply that it only examined the ex-servicemen who had died since returning from the bomb tests. Ninety per cent of the men who had participated in the tests were still alive, although many of them were in ill-health, so I thought their health records should have been looked into. Therefore, the study wasn't really a *study* – it was more of a "statistical survey" which gave no hint of the real human cost or suffering which was involved. This criticism reminded me of the wise words of John F. Kennedy when he signed the Test Ban Treaty in 1963:

> The number of children and grandchildren with cancer in their bones, with leukaemia in their blood, or with poison in their lungs might seem statistically small to some, in comparison with natural health hazards, but this is not a natural health hazard – and it is not a statistical issue. The loss of even one human life, or the malformation of even one baby – who may be born long after we are gone – should be of concern to us all. Our children and grandchildren are not merely statistics towards which we can be indifferent.

Notwithstanding these remarks, the survey was challenged in the *British Medical Journal* by none other than Dr Martin Gardner from Southampton General Hospital who felt that the statistical basis of the survey was open to question.

In early February 1990, Dr Gardner published a paper in the same *British Medical Journal* which looked into the incidence of leukaemia amongst the children of workers from the Sellafield (formerly Windscale) Nuclear Station in Cumbria. The paper caused worldwide controversy, and alarm amongst the nation's nuclear workers, when it claimed to find a link between leukaemia in children and the employment of their fathers in radioactive areas of the plant. This was the first time that anyone had ever stated that a child might develop leukaemia through a genetic flaw in the father's sperm, caused by exposure to radiation.

The 30 January 1988 issue of the *British Medical Journal* contained not only Dr Gardner's paper but also a summarised version of the NRPB report. Dr Gardner, referring directly to the statistical methodology of this report states:

> The authors used service and other records to identify 22,347 men who had been at any of the test locations. About a third

were in each of the Royal Navy, the Royal Air Force, and the Army, and some were civilians working on the nuclear weapons research programme. From independent sources the authors estimated that some 17% of participants, mainly those serving in the Royal Air Force or Army, were not on the original lists and hence were excluded from the study. Some of the Army personnel were missed because their service records had been removed as disability claims had been made. This is unsatisfactory, despite the authors' suggestion from a subanalysis that any resulting bias was small.

I couldn't agree with Dr Gardner's point more. I also noticed a rather strange remark which is contained on page ten of the NRPB report which relates directly to the point made by Dr Gardner. It says:

A total of 1,503 test participants were included in the study who are unlikely to have been exposed to more radiation than the general public. These were individuals whose only visits to the test locations were in the following categories:
(i) Edinburgh Field or Pearce Field, with no evidence of any involvement in cloud sampling or the decontamination of aircraft.
(ii) Monte Bello Islands, but departing before 3 October 1952, the date of Hurricane.
(iii) Christmas Island but departing before 15 May 1957, the date of the first Grapple explosion.
(iv) The crew of HMS Comus or HMS Concord, both of which visited the Monte Bello Islands briefly in March and April 1956 before the first explosion of Mosaic.

In other words, the NRPB study had included over 1,500 men who were never in any danger of being exposed to radiation. They left before the tests started! This group should never have been included in the survey. Their numerical presence merely diluted the results. No doubt this was exactly what was intended.

As far as exposure to radiation goes there were several points worth noting. First, as Dr Gardner says in his letter to the *British Medical Journal*:

Surprisingly little information is given on radiation exposure from the tests since results from personal dosimeters were available for only about 20% of participants.

We all agreed that such a low number surely invalidates any research into the issue. It also leaves rather derelict the claim that we were all issued with badges and that we were all monitored and checked, don't you think?

The report also threw up a rather strange tale of a pilot who received an alarmingly high dose of radiation. It said:

> In one instance a dose of 110 mSv recorded in the Blue Book as having been incurred by a pilot could not be confirmed as no reference to the individual could be found in the health physics records. Neither the squadron's operational record book nor the individual's record of service indicated that he took part in the test in question so the Blue Book entry was assumed to be an error.

After I'd read this section I couldn't help but reflect on the letter I received from the young pilot of the Shackelton which I mentioned earlier. Remember what he said?

> . . . There was torrential rain, which entered the unpressurised aircraft like a sieve, turning the only detector, a small rudimentary device on the captain's lapel, immediately to the wrong colour. I believe another Shackelton was caught in the same predicament . . . .

So, I thought, perhaps the 110 mSv dose which was recorded wasn't a mistake after all. The fact that no reference to the aircraft in question could be found in the official archives didn't surprise me in the slightest, given that lots of ex-servicemen, including me, claim that crucial parts of our medical records have just disappeared.

The NRPB study did not address several issues which could have provided clues and signposts for a more comprehensive health study. For example, the incidence of cataracts amongst the veterans who were still alive should have been examined. This topic merits only the briefest of mentions, on page eighty of the report:

> No information has been obtained about the incidence of cataract, as it does not give rise to a recognisable increase in mortality. This, as far as the authors are aware, is the only somatic disease with a very low fatality rate that is liable to be caused by exposure of adults to moderate doses of radiation.

Whilst no one disputed the validity of this statement we all agreed that cataracts should have been a part of any study carried out into the veterans' health, as early research had already yielded surprising results. The letter sent by Boag *et al* to *The Lancet* said:

> . . . the reported incidence of cataract, virtually unknown as a spontaneous occurrence among young men, is a strong indication that some of those involved had received radiation greatly in excess of a safe dose.

In March 1990 Dr Joseph Rotblat, one of the co-signatories of the above letter to *The Lancet*, told me that, in his personal view, the NRPB's reluctance to study the high levels of cataracts was "most unfortunate". Despite this evidence the incidence of cataracts amongst the servicemen was all but ignored by the NRPB study simply because it didn't kill.

One of the main axes which we had to grind with the report was that it made no attempt to look into the possible genetic effects which exposure to radiation might have had on the servicemen. Many scientists agreed that there was no threshold figure below which exposure to radiation did not produce a genetic effect. I knew for a fact that lots of members of the BNTVA were, like me, sterile. Others had managed to conceive children only to have their hopes dashed when the pregnancy ended in miscarriage. Many had fathered children which had physical or mental deformities. And some simply refused to engage in sexual-intercourse because they feared the worse. All this data I had in my possession should have been enough to force the NRPB into including a health study into the genetic implications of being present during the UK nuclear bomb trials, but it wasn't and it never took place. In the light of the Gardner study into leukaemia amongst the children of Sellafield workers, this refusal to look into the BNTVA's concerns on the genetic issue looks increasingly absurd. What really sticks in my throat, however, was a comment made by an NRPB official during a TV interview shown on BBC TV's *Newsnight* programme in April 1990 when he openly admitted that the NRPB knew all along that a direct link did exist between exposure to radiation and subsequent genetic problems. He said:

> . . . the principle of finding a genetic effect isn't too surprising. Even at very low doses we might get some cells damaged to the extent that they may give rise to cancers twenty or thirty years

after exposure or if it was germ cells you might get genetic damage many years later in future generations.

If this knowledge "wasn't too surprising" then why in the hell did the NRPB not examine the genetic tissue when they looked into the nuclear test veterans? The answer to this question is simple enough: they didn't look into genetics amongst the children of nuclear test veterans because they knew what they'd find.

The NRPB report did make one startling admission in its conclusions, however, when it said:

> Some aspects of the results, however, suggest that a real hazard was associated with the programme. The most striking is the very low probability of finding by chance such large differences as those observed specifically for two diseases for which there were prior reasons for thinking might be particularly likely to be produced . . . On balance, it is concluded that there may well have been small hazards of leukaemia and multiple myeloma associated with participation in the programme . . . the only carcinogenic agent that has been shown to cause an increased incidence of both these diseases is ionising radiation . . .

The NRPB's admission that some of the veterans might have developed either leukaemia or multiple myleloma because of their exposure to ionising radiation during the tests came as no surprise to me and as far as I was concerned it was only the tip of an iceberg. So while the papers ran bleak headlines about the negative implications of the report in relation to our "case" for the future, hardly anyone noticed the references to the higher incidence of these two potentially fatal diseases which, in the NRPB's own words, could exist because:

> . . . the only carcinogenic agent that has been shown to cause an increased incidence of both these diseases is ionising radiation . . .

With some hindsight I feel that the media's shortsightedness wasn't so surprising. If you, the reader, ever stumble upon a copy of the NRPB report I urge you to read between the lines, for you will soon discover that the authors of the report went to extraordinary lengths to bury the results concerning those two diseases. They also did their damnedest to avoid coming to any firm conclusions regarding the causal relationship between participation in the tests and leukaemia or multiple myeloma. This was picked up by Dr Gardner in his letter to *The Lancet* when he said:

> Two particular cancers, however, were significantly higher among participants than among controls – namely, leukaemia (22 deaths against six) and multiple myeloma (six against none). This must be a cause for concern since leukaemia was the first cancer to show an excess among survivors of the Japanese bombs and rates of multiple myeloma rose among them after a latent period of some 15 years . . . . The preferred conclusion so far must surely be that some leukaemias, and probably multiple myelomas, have resulted from radiation exposure during the tests. This is a stronger conclusion than the authors are prepared to reach because of the lack of certainty in the findings.

The authors of the NRPB report even tried to claim that leukaemia and multiple myeloma only showed up higher amongst the veterans because it was uniquely *low* amongst the control group!

The bottom line of the NRPB report is that a link between participation in the tests and subsequent illness amongst the veterans was, in fact, established. The nature of the illnesses are highly significant. Before the report had been written it was widely accepted that if the servicemen had been exposed to radiation then the two illnesses most likely to show up amongst the statistics would be leukaemia and multiple myeloma. That is exactly what happened. But a problem still remained.

The NRPB report shows that both leukaemia and multiple myeloma were more significant amongst the participants' group than the control group. Yet simultaneously, it also states that, according to the sources it used, none of the participants were exposed to particularly dangerous levels of radiation. So, the riddle is this: if the men were safe, then why have many of them died from those two terrible diseases?

To answer that question and unlock the secrets of the NRPB's findings we must backtrack a little. In an earlier chapter we discussed the rain-out theory. I mentioned the 28 April bomb and the rain which followed it. I also provided several witnesses to support my evidence, including the pilot who flew through the rain cloud on the same day. If that rain was irradiated, which I sincerely believe it was, then it would have fallen on various areas of Christmas Island as well. It would have been washed into the lagoons, where we swam and got some of our personal water. Cooking utensils were washed in some of that water too, and we often used it to brush our teeth. The rain would have gone into the sea, where we often caught fish. One man that I know actually saw a friend eat the fish then have a Geiger-counter placed at his fingertips. The reading went off the scale. Ken Taylor, the cook from the island, often served fish and chips to the men, much of which was caught in the local waters, and many men who were there said they'd enjoyed coconuts which they had found near the test site. Both of these could have been radioactively contaminated. Clearly, the rain-out theory points to many of the men being contaminated internally. Even if they had worn them, the only measuring devices and badge-dosimeters which were available at the time would not have been able to measure this type of dose. This is something which the NRPB study itself actually admitted:

> Exposure to neutrons and from internal contamination by radioactive materials will not have been recorded on personal film badge dosimeters.

If the men were contaminated internally via ingestion or inhalation, then this would neatly explain the riddle behind the NRPB's findings.

This hypothesis is supported by more recent findings which were published in the *British Medical Journal* on 5 May 1990. These findings were in a report which examined the New Zealand participants of the nuclear trials in the Pacific. It was, numerically, a smaller study than the NRPB's, but its findings were nevertheless crucially important. Like the NRPB study, it took a group of participants and compared it to a control group of servicemen from the same period. Its findings were most interesting. The study found an excess of leukaemias and multiple myelomas amongst the New Zealand participants. This supports my own personal statistics which I've collated over the years which seem to point strongly in the direction of most leukaemias and multiple myelomas suffered by the servicemen involved having their roots firmly in the later Malden and Christmas Island tests. Interestingly, the New Zealand authors went much further than the NRPB authors in attempting to suggest a possible route by which these two forms of cancer might have gained a foothold without the measuring devices or dosimeter-badges recording high doses. As they say:

> . . . no data are available on internal radiation exposure due to inhalation or ingestion of radioactive particles. The latter may be relevant as the Pukaki and Rotiti visited Christmas Island

after the tests, and it has been hypothesised that rainout into the lagoon and concentration in the food chain could have occurred . . . Thus although currently available data indicate that the Royal New Zealand Navy personnel in Operation Grapple probably received very low doses of gamma radiation, the possibility cannot be excluded that there could have been significant external exposure to neutron radiation or internal exposure due to inhalation or ingestion. There are currently no publicly available data to confirm or refute these hypotheses . . . If these findings are not merely due to chance then they are most likely to be causal rather than due to bias or confounding. Perhaps the strongest reason for concluding that the leukaemia findings may reflect a causal relation is that a similar excess risk was found in the previously published study of British participants in the same nuclear weapons testing programme.

Obviously the results of the New Zealand study were not available to me at the time when the NRPB study was published. Only later would they come to my attention, but the findings completely support my thoughts on the NRPB study. Both studies are significant by themselves but when they are placed side by side, then put into the context of the rain-out theory, their significance increases immeasurably. What they really show of course is that all the measuring devices, scientists and badges, missed the mechanism by which the men were irradiated. No one has ever deciphered how this might have happened. Until now.

But in 1986, when the results of the NRPB study became public knowledge, the association's battle to gain justice for its members became rather messy. This happened for several reasons.

As early as 1986 I knew that we would have to get rid of Section 10 of the Crown Proceedings Act if we were to have any chance of suing the government. This hurdle, as I've explained in the previous chapter, was overcome in 1987. After this victory many members thought that we were on the home straight, a notion which was based on two assumptions. Firstly, we assumed that we could sue retrospectively (i.e. regarding cases of injury or death originating pre-1987). Secondly, we assumed we could find, and support, a veteran who had developed a cancer which was attributable to participation in the bomb tests.

The main obstacle involved the first point. In the Committee Stage of Mr Churchill's Bill, as we've already discussed, the opportunity arose to make the repeal of Section 10 of the Crown Proceedings Act apply retrospectively. This was debated vehemently, with Mr Churchill and Mr Ashley emerging as the two main protagonists. The former opposed the amendment and the latter supported it. After some lengthy discussions, the clause was defeated by eight votes to six. Basically, this meant that any ex-servicemen who thought that they had a case of death or injury originating before 1987 would find it extremely difficult to sue the government for compensation. This obviously had implications for the BNTVA. Any nuclear-test veterans trying to sue the government would have to go through a legal assault course to clear the way for others who might follow. In other words, we needed a test case to make sure the government didn't try to pull a flanker on us by saying that Section 10, since it didn't apply retrospectively remember, could still be invoked as their defence.

The man chosen to act as a test case for other nuclear veterans was Melvyn Pearce. I never met this man personally but I did get to know him through hours of telephone conversations. At all times he came across as a very articulate and highly intelligent person. Melvyn suffered from a rare blood-cancer called lymphoma and he used to spend several days every week on a dialysis machine because his kidneys were seriously damaged as a result of this crippling disease.

Melvyn was a young lance corporal when he watched the nuclear tests on Christmas Island in 1958. Like many other members of the BNTVA he had swum and eaten fruit there during these bomb tests. He also worked close to refrigeration units on the island which were full of radioactive material. At no time did he ever wear protective clothing. Melvyn and I were convinced that his illness was attributable to his service during these nuclear detonations. On this basis the BNTVA drafted in the capable Mr Mark Mildred to act as Melvyn's solicitor. Together we would go through every court in the land to prove that Melvyn and other nuclear test veterans like him had the legal right to sue the government. Our main problem was still the old monolith itself – Section 10. Although it had been flung out in 1987 we knew that it could still be used by the government as a legal defence for cases which involved injury or death pre-1987. It was a pathetic legal technicality providing wafer-thin breathing-space for only the most hard-up and desperate government lawyers who knew they didn't have a leg to stand on.

The first battle ground was the High Court in London. Predictably, the Minister of Defence attempted to use Section 10 as a defence. They said that at the time of his "alleged" exposure to radiation

Melvyn wasn't under the direct care of the army. Lawyers acting for the government insisted that the tests were carried out under the guidance of the defunct United Kingdom Atomic Energy Authority (UKAEA). After the tests were completed, they said, the AEA's authority was transferred to the Secretary of State for Defence. The Secretary of State for Defence could, it was argued, claim "Crown" immunity under Section 10. Ultimately, this third-rate piece of legal shuffling was flung out of the High Court and Mr Justice Caulfield ruled that Melvyn Pearce and the BNTVA had the right to persue this action against George Younger, the then Secretary of State for Defence, and the Ministry of Defence itself.

I was delighted with this decision but I knew that the government wouldn't give up the fight easily. Even though Section 10 was on the way out I was sure the government had it in for the nuclear veterans so I wasn't in the least bit surprised when they went to the Appeals Court.

Mark Mildred prepared his case brilliantly and, to cut a very long story short, the Appeals Court decided in our favour. We thought that this continued public and legal humiliation might have been enough to force the government to back down. I was beginning to wonder how many slaps in the face George Younger could take. But alas, we ended up back in the ring squaring up the MOD lawyers in the highest court in the land . . . the House of Lords. The government and especially George Younger were determined to stop the veterans from going any further with Melvyn's case.

Throughout all this period I didn't have time to think. It was a very tense period for us all and we were told, for obvious reasons, never to discuss our case over the telephone. In quiet moments I would reflect on the situation in which I found myself. Who would ever have believed that Ken McGinley would be playing a major role in a legal battle in the House of Lords, the outcome of which could affect hundreds, perhaps thousands of lives? I certainly didn't.

The night before the Law Lords sat, I was sure we would be beaten by the government's lawyers at the eleventh hour. Journalists called me up and asked me questions all evening. Towards the end of the night I took one call from a gentleman who I shall not identify. He told me in a very calm and clear voice that he knew what the outcome of the Law Lords' decision would be. A very powerful silence suddenly descended on our telephone conversation.

"Well, what's it going to be?" I asked him quietly.

I could almost feel him grinning before he opened his mouth:

"Can you keep a secret? . . . " he said.

"Yes, I can," I replied.

"We've won . . . please don't tell anyone," he said.

I didn't keep this promise very long. After I'd came off the phone I told my wife Alice the good news. When she heard about the decision she just stood there and cried. I began to weep myself.

I was outside the House of Lords the following afternoon to hear the formal announcement of this verdict. When it became public knowledge all hell broke loose. The press headlines screamed that we were on our way to victory and sky-high levels of compensation. But this was in April 1988, three months after the NRPB report had been delivered. That report, as I've already said, listed only leukaemia and multiple myeloma as cancers which were significantly higher in comparison with their "control" group. Melvyn Pearce's disease, lymphoma, was never mentioned.

So, whilst all the celebrations were going on over our victory in the House of Lords, I knew that Melvyn had reached the end of the legal road. This sad reality was eventually brought home in a confidential analysis of his illness which was carried out by Dr Martin Gardner. This study implied that Melvyn's case might, in the light of the NRPB's findings, not be the most suitable for the BNTVA to persue all the way:

> . . . in the A-bomb survivors the lymphomas only accounted for a few percent of the total excess cancers and no significant excess has appeared among the cohorts of workers in the nuclear industry. Therefore, it does seem likely that lymphoma is less readily induced by radiation than, say, leukaemia or myeloma.
>
> We note in the NRPB report that there are no statistically significant excesses of lymphoma among the A-test participants compared to controls in the main analysis nor in the subgroups under study apart from the self-reported cases.
>
> It would seem most unlikely on the balance of probability that this particular case could be shown to be related to radiation exposure from atomic bomb test participation . . .

In the wake of this report and after discussions between Mark Mildred and Melvyn Pearce, the BNTVA decided to shelve plans to take Melvyn's particular case any further. Some commentators at the time regarded this move as an indication that we had given up our fight. Needless to say this was complete nonsense. The association decided to wait until the right moment before it threw weight behind another veteran who was willing to continue with our legal battle. The only condition was that such an individual would have to be suffering from either leukaemia or multiple myeloma, the two cancers highlighted in the NRPB report. This, it was felt, would give us the best chance when it came to the inevitable legal showdown with the government. Legalities aside, I realised that it meant putting a dying man under the scrutiny of government lawyers. By the end of April 1988 I knew that this difficult strategy was our only realistic option. Privately, I couldn't help feeling it was a crying shame.

Mrs Thatcher had always supported her government departments when they answered my letters in negative terms. In one letter, for example, she left me in no doubt about her continued support for the NRPB's findings:

> The NRPB study identified as far as possible, in an unbiased manner, all those who might have been affected by participation in the test programme, and also addressed subsets of those most likely to have been affected by ionising radiation. The study identified no causal link between participation in the test programme and the incidence of cancers among test veterans.

This attitude never surprised me.

But suddenly, almost out of the blue, came the news that two of our members, a widow and an ex-serviceman, had received letters from the DHSS telling them that they were entitled to war pensions. Although both of these people, Mrs Rosslyn Levene from Essex and my old pal Phil Munn, from East Kilbride, had been in touch with the DHSS in the past, they were as shocked as anyone when the good news came through. Both cases had involved individuals who had served on Christmas Island. Mr Leon Levene, Rosslyn's late husband, had served on Christmas Island when he was in the RAF and he'd watched one H-bomb go off in 1957. He died in 1973, aged thirty-six, from leukaemia. Phil Munn, also stationed on Christmas Island during tests in 1958, was also a leukaemia sufferer who underwent daily treatment for his condition. He had previously applied for a war pension on the basis that his condition was attributable to service. He had been turned down.

The letter which Phil received informing him that the original decision had been reversed stated:

> Having considered additional evidence, the Secretary of State
> has now revised the original decision and the Department's
> doctors have advised that the condition of myelo-proliferative
> disease should be accepted as attributable to service.

This letter, from the DHSS remember, appeared to fly in the face of
Mrs Thatcher and the MOD's stated opinion which had said that no
link existed between participation in the tests and subsequent illness.

The "additional evidence" which Phil's letter mentioned was clearly
a reference to the January 1988 NRPB report which had mentioned
leukaemia and myeloma among its findings. The Prime Minister and
one government department, the MOD, were saying that the NRPB
report vindicated their view that no link between participation and
illness existed. Simultaneously, another government department, the
DHSS, was saying that a link had been established and that in Phil's
case, ". . . the Department's doctors have advised that the condition
of myelo-proliferative disease should be accepted as attributable to
service."

It didn't take a genius to work out that a clear conflict between
government departments over this issue had arisen. Official Downing
Street policy was publicly proclaiming the NRPB report proved
nothing whilst another Whitehall department further down the road
was privately writing to nuclear veterans to tell them their illnesses
were attributable to service!

A senior Tory back-bencher who supported our cause immediately
fired off a letter to Social Services Secretary John Moore congratulating
him on his courageous decision to award the pensions in the face of the
Prime Minister's personal opposition. Within a matter of months the
unassailable Mr Moore moved jobs for some strange reason . . .

The fact that the DHSS chose to award these pensions really gave
me heart and I felt that our association was finally being listened
to. Evidently, the government, whether officially or unofficially
(depending which part of Whitehall you stuck a pin in!), had
recognised the two diseases, leukaemia and multiple-myeloma, which
were highlighted in the NRPB's findings. As far as I was concerned this
was a minor victory for the BNTVA and a step in the right direction
towards much greater changes.

In the longer term, however, it was patently clear that the going
would be painfully slow. The only consolation was that the American
veterans under Anthony Guarisco hadn't made rapid progress either.

In fact, in September 1987, after the BNTVA had helped see off Section 10 of the Crown Proceedings Act, I wrote a letter to President Ronald Reagan in the hope that he might get rid of equivalent US legislation which had also stopped servicemen from suing the government. I wrote:

> We are in close contact with the International Alliance of Atomic Veterans and in particular Anthony Guarisco who is their Director. The assistance afforded us by this organisation has been invaluable and they deserve the highest praise.
>
> It has come to our attention that the Feres Doctrine and our Section 10 of the Crown Proceedings Act, 1947, both came into force virtually at the same time. They both served the same purpose – to prevent servicemen, both American and British, suing their Governments for damages for accident or injury caused them whilst serving their countries. After reading various documents it seems to appear that both Governments were unaware of the dangers of low-level ionizing radiation and were determined that servicemen would not have any recourse to justice. To me this is a shoddy and shameful act of the people in power at that time.
>
> I believe the time has now come to redress the balance and I am convinced the Governments of today have a moral and legal obligation to take care of the men who assisted in making our countries great by taking part in nuclear experiments.
>
> We hold an abundance of proof that servicemen were used deliberately to discover the effects of radiation on human beings. I would like to bring to your attention copies of various documents which prove our valid claim:
>
> (1) A letter from the General Counsel of the Department of Defense to the Hon G. V. Montgomery dated 1981. It appears that the persuit of nuclear power and dealings with foreign powers come before the rights of humanity.
>
> (2) The Hearings before the Sub-Committee on Oversight and Investigations of the Committee on Veterans Affairs dated 1983. This document appears to hold the same principals. I note that Gen. Griffiths was dismissed later; I presume because of his incompetence.
>
> (3) De-classified "Top Secret" document dated 1953 which states that men "with and without" protection should be used in the Tests.
>
> (4) A letter to Professor J. S. Mitchell from the Health Physics Division dated 1953 in which it is stated that they needed to know more about the effects of radiation to all parts of the body.

(5) A letter from Admiral Torlesse dated 1951, which was a year before the first British Atom Test. In this he advised that servicemen should be given the benefit of the doubt when it came to proving their illnesses.

. . . Surely in this day and age, when so much has been learned of the awesome effects of radiation, our enlightened leaders should be brave enough to admit that mistakes were made by their predecessors and compensate the victims for the wrong done to them.

I never thought that this letter would do much good but I sent it anyway. By the summer of 1988 I had almost forgotten about its contents and I was sure it had never even reached Reagan. Then I received news from American on 20 May about a historic statement which Ronald Reagan had literally just made. The President announced that he was approving new legislation which would allow US nuclear veterans to automatically qualify for a veterans' pension! Three categories of ex-servicemen were included in this Radiation Exposed Veterans Compensation Act: those who had served with the US forces during the occupation of Hiroshima and Nagasaki; those who were prisoners of war in Hiroshima and Nagasaki; and those who had participated in the atmospheric testing of nuclear weapons. As far as we were concerned it was this third and last category which was the most important. It spelled out victory at last for Anthony Guarisco and all those men who he'd been fighting for throughout the years.

It also gave us a model on which we could build a future strategy based on a similar piece of legislation within a UK context. Such a British Bill would mirror the wording which was included in the US Act which did not attach the blame to any specific party. Nor did it call for a scientifically substantiated link to be found between participation and subsequent illness:

The adjustment applies only with respect to specified diseases – primarily cancer of the various organs – that manifest themselves within 40 years after the veteran last participated in the military radiation-related activity or in the case of leukaemia, 30 years after such participation. Thus, for veterans who served in Hiroshima and Nagasaki or were prisoners of war in Japan, the period for manifestation of the disease has already passed.

The existing fair and equitable system for adjudication of veterans for disability benefits requires demonstration of a connection between a veteran's disability and the veteran's military service. While this legislation bypasses the requirement for demonstration of such a connection, it does so only in specific, narrow circumstances for a truly unique group of veterans.

Enactment of this legislation does not represent a judgement that service-related radiation exposure of veterans covered by the Act in fact caused any disease, nor does it represent endorsement of a principle of permitting veterans to receive benefits funded through veteran programs which bear no relationship to their former military service.

Instead the Act gives due recognition for the unusual service rendered by Americans who participated in military activities involving exposure to radiation generated by the detonation of atomic explosives. The Nation is grateful for their special service and the enactment of [this legislation] makes clear the Nation's continuing concern for their welfare.

The White House,
20 May 1988

When news of this Act became public knowledge, British MPs like Jack Ashley were soon on their feet in the House of Commons asking why, in view of Mrs Thatcher's so-called "special relationship" with the United States, we could not benefit from a similar Bill. But, believe it or not, the intransigence of the government was such that, over a year later, Jack Ashley was still asking exactly the same question:

The Prime Minister claims to have a high regard for service personnel and ex-servicemen. I do not doubt that for a moment, but she should take a hard look at the way which the Ministry of Defence is behaving compared with its equivalent in the United States.

In view of the Prime Minister's close friendship with ex-President Reagan, she should compare his utterances about American nuclear veterans with her own. When signing an Act that provided compensation to American nuclear test veterans one year and two days ago President Reagan said:

"The Act gives due recognition to the unusual service rendered by Americans who participated in military activities involving exposure to radiation generated by the detonation of atomic explosives. The nation is grateful for their special service, and enactments of (the law) makes clear the nation's concern for their continued welfare."

In stark and harsh contrast, the Prime Minister said to me:
"The cause and effect that he says has been proved
has not been proved, and therefore compensation is not
appropriate."

The BNTVA's struggle entered a whole new phase because of the passing of the Act in America. That Act had listed thirteen different types of cancers which, if a veteran had developed any of them, could entitle the ex-serviceman to apply for a war pension. As mentioned earlier, we immediately began to wonder whether it might be possible to put broadly similar legislation on the British statute books. This strategy certainly had several positive points. Firstly, our battle through the courts in the past with Section 10 and then Melvyn Pearce had proved to be difficult. Although we were committed to eventually following through with this approach at some time in the future, we still looked around for alternative options. We also realised that another long legal battle would be costly, lengthy and harrowing for the individual involved. Secondly, we knew we had wide cross-party support in the House of Commons. If this political backing could be used to its full potential then we might be able to put together a Private Member's Bill with similar characteristics to the US Act. This would allow the government off the hook as far as attaching blame went since, like the American legislation, ours would have an in-built "no-fault" clause. Thirdly, we were sure that if such a Private Member's Bill ever reached the floor of the House of Commons, then hopefully the government wouldn't try to oppose it. This attitude might seem naïve but I was praying that, with the advent of television coverage in the House of Commons and in the wake of the government's retreat over war widow's pensions, Mrs Thatcher would, for once, give the nuclear-test veterans the opportunity of a fair hearing.

Within a few weeks I received a call from the BNTVA's Sunderland representative, Mr Mike Reid. Mike said that his local MP, Labour's Bob Clay, was hoping to start work as soon as possible on a Private Member's Bill for us. As you can imagine, I was over the moon with this news and within minutes of receiving it I was on the phone to all the branches to tell them the good news.

Bob went on a fact-finding mission to the United States so that he could study the structure of their Act which Reagan had signed in 1988. He returned with a wealth of detailed background material which would aid him in his attempt to lay the foundations for a Bill in the United Kingdom. I was really optimistic during this period and I kept reflecting on the success of the Private Member's Bill which Winston Churchill had pushed through Parliament, eventually leading to the repeal of Section 10. The more I got to know Bob Clay the more I was sure he could do the same. The last days of 1989 and the first weeks of 1990 saw me on the phone night and day. Bob Clay's efforts appeared to by paying off and my optimism about our chances with his Private Member's Bill were increasing on a daily basis.

I attended a meeting in Blackpool where a member said that he knew someone who might be suitable for our next test case involving a veteran who wanted to sue the government. He said that the gentleman in question, a Mr John Hall from Leicester, would qualify for legal-aid, another factor in the decision-making process which was extremely important given the association's precarious financial position. Mark Mildred and I then contacted John to have a chat about some of his details.

John Hall joined the BNTVA a few years after it was founded. At that time he was in perfect health. He simply joined because he had served on Christmas Island and because he supported the general aims of the association. Some time later he experienced a sudden and dramatic loss of weight. After an appointment with a specialist he was informed that he had a rare form of leukaemia known as "hairy-cell" leukaemia. Four other medical experts advised John that this condition was probably attributable to his service on Christmas Island. Whilst stationed there, he had worked as an RAF aircraft electrician for four months. Afterwards he moved to Adelaide in Australia where he worked on Canberra bombers which had flown through the "mushroom" cloud gathering dust samples after an atomic explosion. At no time during these highly dangerous operations did John wear a respirator. Radiation particles could have been inhaled quite easily by him. If this did happen, even a film-badge measuring external levels would not have helped him.

When I got in touch with John his illness was in its early stages and, apart from extreme bouts of tiredness and daily injections of Interferon, he was in relatively good shape. This was something in our favour since we knew the government would, going on past performances with Section 10 and Melvyn Pearce, do everything in its power to hold up litigation procedures. This bloody-mindedness on the part of the government was, and still is, something I can hardly stomach.

169

As I got to know John Hall better I found him to be a very unique man with a great inner-strength. His background in trade-union matters served him well when it came to the technicalities of dealing with complex legal and political details which inevitably arose after he'd been selected. He was well aware of this and the other main reason why we chose him to be our next legally-backed veteran. John's disease, "hairy-cell" leukaemia, was highlighted in the NRPB findings along with multiple-myeloma. This was obviously to our advantage when we came to the battle with the government in court.

I first met John in a hotel lobby in central London. We chatted briefly then spent some hours with the media who had arrived to film John for the next day's news. Part of the interview involved filming in the hotel bedroom. I asked the hotel manager for permission and explained who we were. I was told to go elsewhere. I explained about John's illness. They still said no. I told them to get stuffed and proceeded to take the BBC crew upstairs. John was asked to wash some dishes in the room's little sink as part of the interview. The cameraman was new and he re-shot the dishwashing scene over and over again. I would have lost my rag after the first two takes, but John Hall just smiled easily and did as he was told. I couldn't help feeling a wee bit humbled in his presence.

The following morning, 1 February, we were up bright and early. After breakfast we caught a taxi to the House of Commons. The man who was driving the cab recognised our badges and said that he wished us the best of luck in our battle with the government.

"You'll need it," he joked with a throaty laugh, "that Maggie's a bleeder! She doesn't give a damn about anyone, not even them that risked their neck for the bleedin' country!"

When we arrived we were greeted outside by other veterans and some MPs. A press conference to announce John's case was held in the Jubilee Rooms, which are next to the Great Hall of Westminster where Parliaments were held in Elizabethan times. John's local MP, Mr Keith Vaz, chaired the conference which was attended by our solicitor Mark Mildred.

The assembled media should not have known John Hall's identity until that morning but a national newspaper had blown the whistle on the story a week before. I'd given them the story at the time on the proviso that they didn't print anything until the morning of the press conference. At the time they'd agreed, so I was really angry when they'd broken this trust. I swore it would never happen again.

Keith Vaz introduced everyone to the media then proceeded to explain how John was going to sue the government on the basis of the legal precedent which had been set some years before by Melvyn Pearce. He also touched on the nature of John's illness, his service on Christmas Island and how his action could be substantiated by the findings of the NRPB report.

Towards the end of the conference Bob Clay said something which made everybody's ears prick up. He announced that he had prepared a Private Member's Bill which, if successful, would give nuclear veterans the automatic right to apply for compensationary pensions. He explained about the American Act on which this Private Member's Bill was based. Winston Churchill from the Conservative Party was also present to offer his support and guidance. They announced that the Bill would receive its Second Reading in the House of Commons on 2 March 1990. Bob Clay, as an experienced Parliamentarian, was fully aware of the difficult nature of the veterans' campaign. He knew that the chances of his Private Member's Bill actually succeeding and becoming law were at best fifty-fifty.

Over the years Mrs Thatcher had gained something of a reputation for being rather cold-hearted on certain issues. I had always felt that our issue fell into this category. But, nevertheless, I agreed with Bob Clay when he decided to write to Mrs Thatcher in an attempt to appeal to her conscience on the matter. This letter was sent prior to the scheduled 2 March Second Reading:

Dear Prime Minister,
Radiation Exposed Crown Employees
(Benefits) Bill

You may already be aware of my proposed Private Member's Bill to introduce benefits for those individuals who, while in Crown Service, were exposed to ionising radiation and may have developed certain cancers and diseases. I write to urge you to give this legislation your fullest personal support.

Since the early 1980s former service personnel and others have campaigned for some modicum of recognition of their plight and the very grave health difficulties faced by some of those who participated in the 21 UK nuclear weapon tests in Australia and the Pacific.

In May 1988, President Reagan approved the introduction of a similar act which provided benefits for American veterans. He did so in a spirit of generosity and compassion. The President said that the American legislation:

"gives due recognition for the unusual service rendered by Americans who participated in military activities involving exposure to radiation generated by the detonation of atomic explosives. The Nation is grateful for their special service and (the Act) makes clear the Nation's continuing concern for their welfare."

Like the American legislation my Bill is not interested in establishing "fault" – it is about compassion. Compassion for a group of people who are now experiencing considerable health problems and dying prematurely and painfully. In 1989 alone, three members of the British Nuclear Test Veterans Association died of leukaemia or multiple-myeloma to say nothing of the many other cancers and diseases suffered.

Of course, I have followed the long debate about medical/scientific/statistical evidence concerning these matters, in particular the NRPB study. I am aware of the progress, or lack of it, that has been made through the Courts by some of those concerned.

As a trained scientist yourself I am sure you would agree that the state of knowledge moves on all the time and it would be a long time, if ever, before there will be a total consensus beyond any doubt on these matters. Possibly, by the time such a consensus emerges all those involved in the 1950s and early 1960s tests will be dead and their dependants also. All the same considerations were weighed by the Senate, Congress and indeed, the President himself and the outcome was the "benefit of the doubt, no-fault, recognition of unique circumstances" Act that President Reagan approved in May 1988. You have said on many occasions that you admire President Reagan. I ask you to emulate the spirit of President Reagan's concern and give your unqualified support to this Bill.

Even if you felt it impossible for the Government to lend positive support I hope you would at least be able to encourage genuine neutrality so that the House of Commons was genuinely free to decide the issue without any adverse tactics being orchestrated by the Government Whips.

Yours sincerely
Bob Clay MP
Sunderland North

After reading this I couldn't help but feel admiration for an MP like Bob Clay, who has no great love for Mrs Thatcher, for having gone to the trouble to write a letter like that. I could see that he was doing his utmost to try and appeal to the humane spirit of the Prime Minister.

He had attempted to use all his considerable powers of persuasion and argument in the hope that she would follow her heart instead of her advisors.

As the date of the Second Reading approached I became more and more optimistic by the minute. Bob was placed second on the running order of Private Member's Bills for Friday 2 March which, relatively speaking, was quite fortunate. The Bill in front of Bob's was the "Planning Permission (Demolition of Houses) Bill" which was also having its Second Reading. It was being proposed by Mr John Wilkinson, a member of the Conservative Party. Although the last paragraph of Bob's letter to Mrs Thatcher had referred to "adverse tactics" I was absolutely certain we would receive a fair hearing.

I'm not ashamed to say I felt some pride when I thought of the length we'd came since my first wee letter to the *Daily Record* in 1982. Over the years we'd lost some brave men to some horrific diseases. But even when we lost them the association still picked up and encouraged their widows to fight on in their names. We had never aligned ourself to any one political party; instead we chose to appeal to the humane side of all politicians. Our fight had started in little halls up and down the country and it had led us to the "Mother of all Parliaments" in the House of Commons. All my life I had respected this place and the laws that it made. Now I, for one day only, wanted some of that respect back.

I travelled down to London the night before the Bill was due to have its Second Reading. I was met by Ken Taylor, Peter Fletcher, Paul Rowles, Archie Ross, Nobby Clark and John Hall. Some widows and the children of deceased nuclear-test veterans were also present. As we took our place in the Strangers Gallery I counted fifteen members in all. The gentlemen who work in the House of Commons recognised our badges and they wished us the best of luck. I took my seat high above the floor of the House of Commons and looked across at the Press Gallery opposite me. It was filled with reporters. I was already anticipating all the good publicity we would get when the veterans Bill was given a successful Second Reading. I felt on top of the world when the debate on Mr Wilkinson's Planning Bill started at 9.37a.m.

As the debate progressed I began to feel a wee bit uneasy and I could feel myself starting to panic. I realised that this debate was unlike any that I'd ever watched on the TV or heard on radio. Usually the speakers are keen to say their bit then get on with whatever's next on the agenda. But that didn't appear to be happening. Any debates that I'd watched were usually straightforward and relatively easy to follow. This one wasn't. By 12.15 I was feeling really uncomfortable. The Minister for Housing and Planning, Mr Michael Spicer, spoke on and on about the Planning Bill. I am no expert but I could see that he was trying to waste time for some reason. A Labour MP opposite him suddenly jumped to his feet:

> *Mr. Don Dixon (Jarrow):* We have not been waffling on like you.
> *Mr. Spicer:* I have only just started, so the Hon. Gentleman has more to come.

When we all heard this we just stared at one another. I felt awful. I felt as if I had let everybody down. The government were clearly doing their best to stop our Bill being debated. To the untrained eye even Mr Deputy Speaker, Sir Paul Dean, appeared to side with them. The Labour MP Dennis Skinner got to his feet:

> On a point of order, Mr Deputy Speaker. The Minister is replying to a debate in which all the Hon. Members who have spoken support the Bill. The Minister has now been speaking for more than half an hour, and it is evident to some of us that he is stretching matters. I was about to use the word "filibuster", but you would not like that. Standing Order No. 35 deals with the matter of the Question being now put. It says:
> "unless it shall appear to the chair that such motion is an abuse of the rules of the House, or an infringement of the rights of the minority, the question 'That the question be now put' shall be put forthwith."
> No one has spoken against the Bill. The next Bill on today's agenda is about looking after people who are dying from cancer because they were in the vicinity of nuclear tests in the Pacific. It is promoted by my Hon. Friend the Member for Sunderland, North . . . .

And so it went on and on. By 1p.m. it was clear that we were getting nowhere. I began to feel physically sick as I listened to Conservative MP after Conservative MP stand up and talk absolute nonsense just to waste time. One member in the particular, Mr James Arbuthnot, the Conservative member for Wanstead and Woodford, sticks out in my mind:

Mr. Bob Cryer (Bradford South): Could not that point be argued just as effectively in Committee, so that those whose freedom has been interfered with by radioactivity poisoning could be satisfied that the House is considering the awarding of proper and adequate compensation through the Radiation Exposed Crown Employees (Benefits) Bill? That Bill is due to be considered next, but the Hon. Gentleman seems intent on not talking about it.

Mr. Arbuthnot: I have not been thinking about the Bill that is to follow. If we reach it in time, that is fine . . .

Mr. Allan Rogers (Rhondda): The Hon. Gentleman has cast aspersions on my Hon. Friend's feelings about freedom. Does the Hon. Gentleman feel no loyalty to former servicemen who are dying of cancer as a result of being poisoned while carrying out their duties in Australia and elsewhere? Is he entirely happy for them and their widows to be deprived of their fair dos? He has plainly been set up as a stooge to talk the Bill out. Does not participating in such an exercise make him feel a little dirty?

All the time that this banter was going on I could see some of our members were beginning to get really upset. I didn't know what to do. I was out of my depth. I looked down to Bob Clay who was almost white with anger and frustration. He looked up at the members and the widows with their children. He stood up to speak:

Mr. Bob Clay (Sunderland North): On a point of order, Mr. Deputy Speaker. You will know that I have been in the Chamber all morning and that up to now I have not made any points of order or intervened. The last thing that I want to do is hold up proceedings. However, as someone who is not a procedural expert, may I put it to you, Mr. Deputy Speaker, that the Hon. Member for Wanstead and Woodford [Mr. Arbuthnot] has now been speaking for 20 minutes, after many other long speeches, including one of 45 minutes from the Minister?

I should like to put it to you and, through you, to some Conservative Members, that many people outside the House will not understand these parliamentary games and the British ex-servicemen and their families who had enormous hopes of the Bill that is to follow this Bill will be appalled if the House fails to pass that Bill, and even more appalled if there is not even the opportunity to discuss it and to have something put on the record. I listened carefully to what you said in response to earlier points of order but I urge you, Mr. Deputy Speaker, to facilitate whatever moves you can to allow those who have come here today to listen to our discussions about a Bill that is about people who are dying and who fear dying, who cannot wait another year, two years or 10 years for the legislation, and who should have an opportunity to be heard.

Bob's words almost brought tears to my eyes. I knew that he was doing his level best to turn the whole disaster around and salvage something in the last hour of Parliamentary time which was left. Just as he finished his remarks the proposer of the first Planning Bill, the Conservative MP Mr Wilkinson, made an astonishing offer to lose his own Bill so that ours could be debated.

Mr Wilkinson: Further to that point of order, Mr. Deputy Speaker. I hereby forgo any rights which, by the leave of the House, I may have to reply to the debate and I beg to move, that the Question be now put –

I was delighted when I heard this. I was sure Mr Deputy Speaker would accept his humane offer and move on to the next Bill which of course was ours. But no, the Speaker had other ideas:

Mr. Deputy Speaker: I am not prepared to accept that motion.

I was in a hell of a state when I heard this. It was bad enough watching the Tory MPs demolish years of hard work in such a humiliating fashion, but to have to watch Mr Deputy Speaker encouraging them was sickening. The Labour MPs were up in arms and they did their best to convince the Speaker that he'd made a mistake:

Mr. Roland Boyes (Houghton and Washington): Further to that point of order, Mr. Deputy Speaker. Are you taking into consideration the fact that it is the Bill's promoter . . . who has moved the closure and has asked that the Question now be put? Surely, if the Hon. Gentleman is honourable enough to give my Hon. Friend the Member for Sunderland, North [Mr Clay] at least the opportunity to speak to his Bill – although we hope that it will receive its Second Reading today – should you not take the fact that the Hon. Gentleman has made that gesture into account when considering the closure?

Mr Deputy Speaker wouldn't take any notice. Time after time he called Mr Arbuthnot to his feet. We watched this horrific pantomime with a mixture of physical and emotional disgust. The whole thing went beyond a joke when another comic-cut Conservative started his speech:

> I have serious reservations about my Hon. Friend's Bill. I shall begin by going back in time and examining the way in which a human settlement develops over the centuries.
>
> I take as an example Southwark, on the south bank of the Thames. One can find evidence of a settlement there going back 2,000 years. The Romans used the same area for further building, and throughout the dark ages, the Norman conquest and mediaeval times . . . .

At this point we'd had enough. We had sat in the Strangers Gallery for over five hours watching brilliant men like Bob Clay and Dennis Skinner plead with other human beings to listen to reason on the basis of compassion. It was enough to make the calmest of men lose the rag.

As the fifteen of us stood up to leave I looked down at the Chamber of the House of Commons for the last time. Mr Michael Spicer, the government's Minister for Housing and Planning, was lounging with his feet up on the bench in front of him. He looked straight up at the Strangers Gallery. My gaze met his. For one awful moment I got the distinct impression that he was laughing. I looked away, gritted my teeth and followed the rest of the veterans out.

The delegation went down to the Central Lobby of the Commons where we were met by Mr Boyes from the Labour Party. He listened to our complaints and went back inside to put them on the record in the last minute of the debate:

> *Mr. Boyes:* I have just been outside to the Central Lobby to talk to the nuclear veterans. They are disgusted at the performance of Conservative Members and find it an absolute disgrace. All those who have filibustered today should be ashamed of themselves.

One of our members, Archie Ross, was so angry that he sent a note into the Chamber requesting an interview with Mr Arbuthnot who had filibustered our Bill. The reply came back within minutes. The little handwritten note said:

177

It would not be right for me to see a non-constituent in the lobby.

I read this and shook my head. I was speechless. I had to help a fellow veteran, Peter Fletcher, into a taxi outside the Commons that afternoon. He was sobbing his heart out. My eyes filled up with tears as well. It was a pathetic and disturbing end to a humiliating day.

The national newspapers had headlines the next morning which reflected our anger. The Scottish *Daily Record* which had been the first newspaper in Britain to highlight our cause said:

TORIES KILL A-BOMB BILL

Army veterans hit by cancer from atom bomb tests were kicked in the teeth by Tory MPs yesterday. Moves to compensate the ex-serviceman failed after Government backed time-wasting in the Commons. Labour's Bob Clay had brought in a Private Member's Bill in a bid to get automatic damages for veterans of the Christmas Island tests . . . The Sunderland MPs move had all-party support – including the backing of Tory MP Winston Churchill. But the Government blocked it by talking out Commons business . . . Furious Bob Clay blasted last night: "Those Tory MPs who did the Government's dirty work will have this on their conscience for the rest of their lives."

Bob was determined to keep going and a few weeks later I received word that his Private Member's Bill was being "tagged on" to a Labour Social Security Bill due to be heard on 28 March. I had vowed to journalists after the 2 March debacle that I would never again set foot in the House of Commons. I was true to my word and I refused to go down to London on the 28th. But, even after the terrible events involving the 2 March sitting I still hoped that we might have an outside chance with the 28 March reading. I should have known better.

The main problem was the fact that the government were determined to stop the debate going on any longer than it had to. To do this they employed the time-stopping "Guillotine" motion. The debate had to end at 1a.m.

Bob Clay, as usual, introduced the issue brilliantly. At 12.30a.m. he said:

These people believed that they were serving their country. This issue has nothing to do with one's view on nuclear weapons. If, like me, one is totally opposed to their possession, one obviously takes the view that it is horrific that people would have contracted these terrible diseases while participating in the testing of them. If, like many Conservative Members, one believes that nuclear weapons have kept the peace for many years, one should be all the more grateful to those servicemen who participated in the programme to test them. This is not a pro or anti-nuclear weapon issue. It is an issue of basic justice.

The Under-Secretary for Health, Mrs Gillian Shephard, put forward the government's case. As usual she went over all the old ground about the issue. She said the tests were safe, everyone in danger had worn a dosimeter and that the government had commissioned an independent study by the NRPB who had found no evidence of any link between participation in the tests and illness among servicemen. Appeals to the compassionate side of Mrs Thatcher's party had obviously fallen on deaf ears. By the time she'd finished speaking it was clear that the Bill's supporters were never going to have enough time to show up the transparent nature of the government's wafer-thin defence over the issue. At 1a.m. the House divided. Minutes later the result of the voting was delivered. We were defeated by 276 votes to 218. Among those who voted against our Bill were Edwina Currie, Kenneth Baker, Norman Fowler and, surprise surprise, our old friend Mr James Arbuthnot.

When I heard about our defeat I wasn't really so surprised. In many ways I felt more sorry for Bob Clay – it was him who had done all the hard work. I knew that all the members would be sad as well but they'd live with it the same way they live with pain every day of their lives. I just sat at home in the early hours of the morning looking at a small note I'd received through the post on the day the Bill was due to be read. The message was handwritten on a sheet of House of Commons notepaper. It said:

Dear Mr McGinley,
    The Government have today announced a guillotine on the Social Security Bill which makes it more difficult for the Nuclear Test Veterans case to be heard.
    I have no doubt that this is quite deliberate.
    I will certainly join other colleagues in doing what I can to prevent further cheating of proper discussion.

That note had arrived on the morning of the 28 March debate. The author hadn't signed it.

I wasn't bitter about the March 1990 events in the House of Commons. On reflection I knew that I'd learned something. If the government went to all that trouble to stifle and silence our argument, then it means we have a credible case. It also confirmed my long-standing belief that the government of the United Kingdom has something to hide.

Chapter Eight

MY HEART TELLS me that I should keep going, constantly trying to convince you about the validity of the veterans' case but my head tells me I'll soon run out of pages. So, I ask myself, how do I end a story like this? The short answer is that I can't.

The nuclear tests that I, and thousands of other ex-servicemen and unsuspecting civilians, witnessed in the 1950s and 1960s, were a crime against humanity. The documents that I've presented in this book show that the criminals, the government of the United Kingdom, knew what the consequences of these premeditated acts would be. Death, usually in the form of cancer, would creep up decades after the tests had taken place. The criminals would be long gone by that time and they covered their tracks well. Anyone trying to unearth the facts pertaining to the nuclear tests was always going to have a hell of a task. Many documents on the subject are classified until the year 2000 and beyond, a fact which speaks for itself.

But it doesn't end there. Although I've walked into one bureaucratic brick-wall after another I will never stop fighting for the nuclear test veterans. For it is this group of men who are the real victims of the crime. We were all regarded as nothing more than idiotic lumps of flesh in uniforms who were worth nothing. Our value lay only in our biological and psychological potential as subjects in experiments with radiation. Once the tests had been carried out and the scientists had gathered their data, the authorities disappeared leaving the men to pick up the pieces. But their actions left a stain. Those young soldiers were warm, intelligent, loving, humorous and caring individuals who knew something was wrong in their lives. They told friends, relatives and loved ones about their fears. The whispers became conversations, the conversations became meetings filled with angry voices and eventually the whole country knew about the illnesses that these men were suffering from. Then, after the BNTVA was founded, the government tried to stall us with excuses. When that failed they used the lowest legal defences available. When those failed they employed half a dozen spineless stooges to utilise cowardly Parliamentary practices to block our way in the House of Commons. They will stop at nothing to see us off.

There have been plenty of nights when I thought about giving the association up, but the next morning I've always came down the stairs to find the postman has delivered another pile of letters for me. This correspondence might come from widows, children of servicemen or ex-soldiers themselves. The letters rip your heart out when you read them. They come from decent, sincere and ordinary people who have been handed a horrific legacy by the government. Only a cold-hearted monster could ignore their pleas for help. I'm nothing special but I try to read each one and reply as soon as possible. All my replies reflect my innate optimism which tells me justice will be done one day. That's why this story can have no ending. Here's a selection of those I've received:

> My husband Ken Lewis was chosen to be one of the crew of the first Valiant V-Bomber, and was at Wisley at the Vickers works in Weybridge. Eventually the crew brought the aircraft to RAF Wittering – the aircraft being put behind screens as it was "Top Security" with boffins working with the crew. As it was a Top Security project, wives were not given, nor did we expect, any information what the men were about to do. However, we were not stupid! After a while Bob Bates and crew brought another Valiant to Wittering. These two crews did all the initial tests and trials. They were 1321 Flight. W. Hubbard joined them and 49 Squadron was formed. This squadron went to Christmas Island to test the H-bomb, so it was pretty obvious what they were doing behind those screens. [After his return] My husband developed severe back trouble which was diagnosed as arthritis. However, the X-ray showed two broken ribs and crumbling back bones. He was given a corset which did nothing to help. He was seen by various departments and doctors over a period of 9 months and given nothing to help the pain which became intense. He was referred to the Haematology Dept. where he was diagnosed as having multiple myeloma and was given a period of chemotherapy which did help him (I shall be eternally grateful to these people). He developed chronic diarrhoea and was given a colostomy, which was replaced after some weeks. The surgeon reported that Ken had cancer of the liver (we decided not to tell him). The chronic diarrhoea returned. He was given another colostomy

and a course of radiation treatment. The surgeon reported Ken now had cancer of the lungs (which we did not tell him). His condition deteriorated very quickly and he died before the colostomy could be replaced. When we travelled abroad Ken always set the alarm bells off although he had no metal objects on his person. His height went from over 6 feet tall to just over five feet owing to the crumbling backbone. The chap from the other Valiant, Bill Bates, died later from leukaemia.

Love,
Jo

Please let me say thank you for attending John's funeral . . . you already know how disgusted and angry I am but I am even more so now since reading the so-called experts' views on the subject of genetics. They knew right from the start how this would affect the future generations of the boys who served during the tests. My whole world has been shattered by the death of John at such an early age, now I feel I have been left a terrible legacy of a mentally handicapped daughter and another daughter with a slight disfigurement of the leg all due to his service to his country on Christmas Island. I feel this government is just passing the buck from one government department to another; why oh why do they do this Ken? Surely in the end they must recognise that they did wrong and publicly say so.

Kind Regards,
Emily

. . . he was on the island for two months . . . after coming back from the bomb-site he did blackout and was carried back to the sick-bay where he remained unconscious for two days. His repatriation back to England was with two male nurses in attendance, there was no mention of that in [his medical records]. They also failed to say that there was an ambulance waiting for him on the tarmac at Heathrow to take him to Uxbridge Hospital . . . Tests were taken at Uxbridge Hospital, then he was taken to Holten Hospital and tests were carried out for over *two months*. Neither hospital let his family know where he was so it was obvious he was too ill to let us know . . . He is 63 years old now and the past 30 years have been hell for him. He has never had sex with his wife because he is sterile . . . Also his gums used to bleed a lot then he lost all his teeth, he's had lots of nose bleeds, he's lost his hair, he's lost his finger and toe-nails and he carries burn marks all over his body.

Your,
Doris

NO RISK INVOLVED

Not long after our marriage I discovered he had served
on Christmas Island during the nuclear tests, which were
conducted by the Americans in 1962. He consistently talked
about Christmas Island and of his experiences, witnessing a large
number of Atomic Bombs. When we had thunder and lightning
storms . . . his behaviour was very irrational . . . he also suffered
agonizing stomach pains and became violently ill after each storm
. . . For some months he would remain in good spirits, then after
having bad nightmares about Christmas Island, he would talk
non-stop about atomic bombs. He would then resign from his
job to get away from it all. I remember one time . . . after a
thunder and lightning storm [he] started shaking violently and
could not control himself for ten minutes. He seemed to be in
a state of shock and we had to lift him onto the lounge chair.
Again it went back to Christmas Island and the atomic bombs.
He was on tranquillizers for weeks after that episode.

In 1958 my husband was one of the servicemen who took part
in the Nuclear Test Trials on Christmas Island. 30 years later his
life came to a premature end at the age of 50, after developing
malignant melanoma . . . Vic never spoke much about it and
although we would have been married 29 years this September,
the photos I found after his death shook me up a bit, as I've never
seen them before. I can't think where he had tucked them away
and now I shall never know . . . As you can guess I miss Vic
desperately and would give anything to have him back again, but
alas, that can never be. He loved life and I have some fabulous
memories to hang on to. Fortunately we had a good life together
and three lovely daughters who worshipped him. I'm very glad
in a way that he didn't suffer any longer than he did as it was
too distressing for us all to see him fading away to nothing after
he had been so full of life. At least he's at peace now.

Love,
Sylvia

I have a friend whose sons are in the army and she has always
known, weeks and often months in advance where they were to
be stationed to do tours of duty. For a few of us it is so easy to
remember how different things were in the fifties; and I feel it is
important that others should try and visualise it all as it *was*, so
that they can understand . . . When Roger came home on leave
we knew he was going abroad . . . Roger and I were babies and
young children during the war – "too young to remember" – that
you didn't talk about such things as movement of troops. We did

remember though. It had been trained in us; and in the same way we, not them, had to accept being called up on National Service. So when my husband-to-be shipped off back to camp that Sunday evening I did not know where he was going. It was with profound relief that I heard when he left the country that it was not to war.

When he returned Roger was a different man. He tried so hard to fit in but he was ill and he never really recovered. He was given "time to settle", and I remember his dentist, a sailing club friend of our parents, recognised how desperately ill he was and tried to convince Roger's mother. Her reaction was not just indignant; it was vicious. Mental illness was a stigma in those days, Roger was diagnosed as schizophrenic but he discharged himself from the nursing home and it was kept a secret, so secret that I was not told after, let alone before I married him. I honestly did not know until after he died. I found out bits during our married life – only ever at night, never in the cold light of day. I have put them all together since but I did not realise the agonies he must have suffered [for] he died a hypermaniac and schizophrenic . . . I asked him several times what the big red/brown areas were on his back and side "Were they birth marks or something?" "No, I don't know – just Christmas Island," he would always reply. He never took his shirt off even in the garden on the hottest day in case someone saw the marks.

When he came home they found among other things he had Addison's Disease [lack of Adrenalin] and needed all his teeth out . . . they put him in hospital and pumped him full of adrenalin; then pulled his teeth out . . . the pain was quite indescribable . . . I know he would speak to no one for 24 hours and just snarled at the nurses, cursing and swearing if they went near him. It was often that he went quiet and it was as though somehow it was the last straw. They had told him that the bomb had made him sterile and he could never have children . . . They had told him he was a schizophrenic – a nut-case. He had to carry a card in his wallet in case he had an accident and needed steroid treatment. He often didn't carry it because he felt so ashamed. He felt Christmas Island had made him half a man and I was never allowed to mention to anyone that he had been there. When I conceived they just didn't believe it was his child – even his mother's first words were "Well at least its got the [family's] shaped head". The relief showed in her face that my husband wasn't saddled with a bastard son, but I wasn't allowed visitors to see us. When my second son threatened to miscarry she even accused me of trying to get rid of it because of

the possibilities resulting from Christmas Island. In fact no such
danger had ever occurred to me.

Andrew, my first born, was born with two thumbs on one
hand. My mother-in-law insisted on the doctor tying one off
before Roger saw it, and it was cut off a few days later as he
lay in his basket beside my bed. I had all three sons at home
because Roger had said he could not bear even to visit after
his experiences in hospital. In the 6 weeks spent in hospital
when David threatened to miscarry he only visited me once.
(I had five miscarriages altogether) . . . When I found he
was taking his cortisone as pep-pills at the rate of six or
more a day I got the doctor to speak to him but they still
didn't tell me he was schizophrenic and should have been on
other pills as well. He shirked all responsibility and was out
every single night, spending his money on beer, also a phase
of horses and latterly motor-bikes. I think these brought him
relief from what he felt was the shame of himself as a result of
Christmas Island.

When Robbie was born I was desperate for money; we were
knee-deep in debt and I was not given enough even for food.
My mother gave me a £100 and I started a market stall selling
hand crocheted goods. Within a year I opened my own shop
and that had to keep us going. Roger was often increasingly
violent . . . Anyway to cut a long story short he went into the
bathroom one night when the boys were in the bath and I found
the three children crying when I went up to say goodnight. I had
done my utmost to shield them when Roger had a bad phase but
quite suddenly I asked if they wanted to leave and they said yes.
So next day, after 14 years of marriage I went to put my name
down for a house on the same co-ownership estate on which we
lived and within three weeks we moved down the road. I'd never
had new furniture, it was all cast offs and second hand so I just
started with the cast offs again.

After that Roger went to pieces. He was absent sometimes
from work and would be outside my house around the back at
night. He thought he was being followed because he worked for
Rolls Royce and Associates on nuclear submarine drawings and
when he visited one time it grieved me because the children
laughed about him. I'd left him in August. It was not really
surprising when I was visited by his section leader at the
beginning of October to tell me that they had to persuade
him into an ambulance and he was in the mental hospital in
Derby. I visited him and I have high praise for the staff at the
hospital . . . On the last Saturday in January he came as he had
often done, to lunch. When I had to go back to the shop he came

out to the car with me and made me promise that I would always look after the children. I assured him I would and he went inside and watched TV for a while with them. I had expected him for tea but he didn't come. It sounds melodramatic now but I know that if I had visited him that evening he would have killed me as well as himself. As it was, he hanged himself from the rafters on Sunday morning.

After he died the neighbours blamed me for leaving him I suppose and I suffered car tyres being damaged, mud thrown on my windows and door, people calmly walking across my garden to get to the field behind and anonymous phone-calls . . . My eldest son wanted to be in the air force but they wouldn't have him. I took him to the only hand specialist in the country and he assured me it was nonsense that the air force would not have this cadet because of his hand. Christmas Island had cast its shadows again . . . He now has a first class honours degree in engineering.

When they exploded the bomb on Christmas Island it was as though they blew a part of Roger's life away with it. But if, through the horrors of those tests future generations realise the folly of blowing holes in the stratosphere and showering the planet with nuclear waste then – please God – my husband will not have died in vain.

My husband Major General Denis Moore was chosen to be the army representative to witness a nuclear test on Christmas Island in 1957 . . . The test was to be of a megaton bomb (high air burst I would imagine) the most powerful device existing at that time. Certain aspects of this event made a profound impression on my husband, and on his return from Christmas Island he talked to me at length of his experiences.

Some ten minutes before the explosion was timed to take place the three service representatives were required to take their places seated in a row on the bare turf of the island floor. It was explained to them that they were facing away from the area in which the explosion was to take place, and they were situated at a distance of some twelve miles from this spot. They were required to cover their eyes with their hands. After a short elapse of time the instruction came to face about and unshield their eyes. I imagine the roar of the explosion reached them some moments later, but my husband did not mention this. He was entirely rivetted by the sight before him . . . Hours after the explosion they were taken up in a light aircraft to view the devastation wrought by this great blast. He spoke of the widespread desolation they looked down on – miles and miles of bare brown ground stripped of all vegetation except for the occasional stark tree trunk rearing up from the scorched earth. They were evidently flying close to the ground, for he was greatly moved by the sight of live birds entirely denuded of feathers wandering on this desolate surface. These luckless flightless creatures doubtless blinded by the blast, were seen to be blundering aimlessly over the waste. The sight made a vivid impression on him and he could not forget it. On a later airborne survey of the site all traces of wildlife had gone.

[My husband] died in March 1987. Symptoms of radiation effects only became evidenced in 1982 and consisted of a long series of septic conditions of varying severity. His case was of considerable interests to the haematologists who finally diagnosed a blood condition known as myeloma or cancer of the bone marrow. Three separate inquests were performed on him and the coroner had considerable difficulty in attributing the cause of death to radiation effects. He spoke to me after the final inquiry, at which he returned an open verdict, explaining that the length of time between exposure and the onset of symptoms was too long to be typical. Thus I had little hope of obtaining compensation although I am myself convinced that his condition was indeed due to his experience on Christmas Island. Myeloma is a specified result of radiation contamination and accounted for all his symptoms . . . Some blame for the illness and death of so many of our servicemen must be laid at the door of the medical, scientific and weaponry experts whose complacence in the 1950s went unchallenged.

Another woman wrote to me about her husband who had recently died. She said that he'd always maintained he'd never live to see fifty. He died aged forty-six. After his passing she examined his personal possessions and discovered a small drawing that he'd made during his participation in the bomb tests. The sketch was on a little note-pad, similar to a school jotter. The picture is headed "Christmas Island Nov 8 '57 – H Bomb Tests". The illustration is dominated by a large mushroom cloud after a nuclear test. On the right-hand side is a grapnel bird symbolising Operation Grapple, whilst on the left we find a small land-crab. But down in the corner is the most macabre part of the otherwise innocent-looking drawing, for here we find the small, perfectly drawn image of a human skeleton.

I also received a letter from the sister of one of the very first victims of Christmas Island. Sapper William 'Billy' Friar Morris went there in the same year I did, 1958. He was twenty years old and was passed A1 in the army's physical fitness test. After witnessing an A-bomb blast he was taken to America for medical treatment. He was discharged from the army soon after, on medical grounds. After returning home his girlfriend became pregnant. She later suffered a miscarriage. Within six months of returning from Christmas Island Sapper Morris was dead. Quantities of the radioactive Strontium 90 (this substance was in the news after the Windscale disaster) were found in his young body. His sister wrote:

> . . . the government should have admitted liability. No amount of money can bring my brother's life back but the government should honour the young lives that were lost due to their experiments . . . I can remember the day the telegram came to say my brother was being discharged from the army through ill health "On Medical Grounds" as they put it, we couldn't believe it.

One piece of correspondence I received came from Mr Collins. It said:

> During 1957 to 1958 I was stationed on Christmas Island in the South Pacific. I was responsible along with Frank Gornall from Garton in Manchester (who as about 20-21 years also) for installing a number of Bendix washing machines to be used for the washing of radioactive clothing worn by the technicians working on the island. These machines were all "wasted" into one big filter and the water emptied into a six-foot iron disposal pipe about 1/4 mile away from the machines. This pipe emptied semi-horizontally into a pit which had a permanent amount of water in it. Surrounding the pit were notices saying "Danger Radioactive Material" but it was not fenced off. The officer in charge didn't like the fact that the pipe emptied semi-horizontally into the pit and the water overflowed and could splash back out, so he asked us to modify it. This involved stripping the pipe back about 20 feet or so to the next joint and adding a new piece of pipe with an elbow and down pipe dipping into the water. This "down pipe" also had to be drilled so that the water also sprinkled out "shower" fashion from the bottom.
> The ground around the pit was sand and whilst we were doing this work the ground collapsed and I slid into the pit grabbing hold of the pipe to stop me going under completely. I was submerged in this water up to my chest though and scrambled

out with the help of Frank. I was then taken to a medical centre tent by Frank in the landrover and here I was scrubbed by three medics with soap and water. I was tested with a Geiger-counter and re-scrubbed and re-showered for a few hours until eventually the counter reading was safe. I didn't sign any sheets and neither was I given instructions to return for further tests, I was just sent back to camp and told to return to normal duties. I don't recall if Frank was tested as well.

There was also a second incident where I was one of the 25 *not* evacuated when G.B. tested the largest megaton bomb. All other personnel were evacuated by boat for the day.

Our job was to sandbag the doorways up to the testing stations and then take refuge in an "elephant shelter" while the blast took place. After an hour or so when the heat had subsided we had to unsandbag the doorways so that the scientists could return. We did not wear special clothing of any sort . . . we were all issued with a litmus-type paper testing-badge for re-entry and told that should it change colour we had to immediately inform our senior officers. The procession for re-entry was three landrovers, a 3-tonner and a further three landrovers. I was returning to the blast zone in the 3-tonner but for some reason I was ordered to get into the third landrover and operate a Geiger counter whilst the senior officer drove. I was told to set the meter to zero and then inform the senior officer should the needle enter the red-zone. I received a dangerous reading and the procession was stopped whilst the scientists returned and tested the area. They stated that the reading was inaccurate because I was using the counter wrongly so we continued on our way and completed the removal of the sandbags.

Signed:
J. Collins
Witness:
J. O'Kane

This tale of ineptitude and neglect was one of the most harrowing that I'd ever read in all my years as Chairman of the BNTVA. What makes it all the more tragic is the fact that, believe or not, you have read a death-bed statement. Mr Collins, you see, dictated this letter in September 1987 some three weeks before he died from cancerous tumours which had spread throughout his body.

And so it goes on. Day after day I open letters. Day after day I answer the telephone to take calls from ex-servicemen, widows and their children. I do my best to answer their questions. My heart goes out to all of them, especially the children. The crime against them all was committed years and years ago but, as old and new research keeps proving, the genetic legacy will be passed on from generation to generation. Every person touched by the nuclear tests has a story which deserves to be heard. The government will only class them as "statistics" in their surveys, but to me they mean more than that. They are human-beings and I know that each and every one of them gives me the courage to keep fighting on, on their behalf. In that sense they aren't victims – they're heroes. The words of journalist John Pilger sum up my feelings towards them:

> They are people frequently lost in the broad sweep that is the nature of much television and print journalism; they are dismissed as the minutiae of a news story when, in truth, they are really the story. Or they are portrayed merely as victims when, in truth, their courage and resilience are often heroic.

This book has not sought to establish itself as a definitive historic, scientific or military account of the nuclear bomb trials of the 1950s and 1960s. I would never tackle such a project and in many ways I wouldn't want to. Academic research would only confirm my view that the UK's whole atomic programme, from the Windscale disaster which was inadvertently caused by the reckless rush to produce military-grade Plutonium for the nuclear tests on Christmas Island and elsewhere, to the actual tests themselves, amounted to nothing more than a tragic pantomime from start to finish.

I want to live long enough to see the government admit that mistakes were made and pay out compensation to all the victims of the nuclear tests. I want to see the hundreds of widows who watched their husbands slipping away have their cases heard so that they might live a little easier with the terrible pain which comes with losing a spouse. But more important of all, I want to watch all the children born into a life of pain and misery because their fathers participated in those tests, be looked after by the authorities of this land who, after all, are the real criminals.

As for me? Well, I don't really care. I'm not as young as I used to be and my only real pleasure these days comes from spending time with my wife and my daughter. The rest of my life is built around the BNTVA and in a way I suppose, it's become an obsession. I take each day as it comes and I never look too far ahead. Any doubts or fears that I have usually come last thing at night when

I'm lying on my bed. I worry about whether or not I've taken on too big a task. I worry about the health of all the veterans. I worry about the sender of that tragic letter I received the day before. I worry about my health and my wife and child too. But then I close my eyes tightly, the way I did when I was just a boy in the army, and I say my prayers to myself. I know that this faith will see me through the way that it's always done. I know that someone, somewhere is listening to me.